Infamous Roman Emperors

Conquest, Sabotage, and Betrayal
in the Roman Empire

August Mead

Table of Contents

Introduction

Across the protracted annals of history, there appear numerous pinnacles, beacons of exceptional occurrences that stand out among the more mundane inserts. Moments where the brilliant efforts of extraordinary people or groups rose to shine through the years after they happened. Periods when the world was illuminated by innovation and leadership. Nations birthed from nothing to become earth-shakers and culture-formers. Those crests of magnificence define the ages, each epoch radiating in what they have given to the world.

Ancient civilizations expanded, growing beyond the walls of their small clay cities to accumulate more wealth, more land, and more power. Be it through war, blood, scheming, or diplomacy, each one forged into new territories, conquering until borders were extended further and further. Every nation flexed its muscles as rulers sought to make their mark and become immortalized in stone statues and gold coins. Along with this power and dominance came new cultures, inventions, and improvements that would also stand tall as reminders of their moment in the spotlight.

Egypt emerged from the burning sands under the grandeur of the Pharaohs. Their gifts of a complex writing system and monumental pyramids stand as testimonies to an era of greatness. With the likes of Ramses and Cleopatra, the rule of the desert people made a searing mark on the chronological timeline. Greece also had its time in the sun, basking in democracy, and philosophy as Alexander the Great spread his rule across the map. Olympics and theater were among many of the new additions they offered society.

Not to be outdone in the Far East, Chinese dynasties rose to bring numerous inventions to light while battling against a mounting Mongol empire under Ghengis and Kublai. Persia's influence on human rights was felt for eons through the reign of Cyrus and Xerxes. And, far across the seas, the Mayans 'contributions to astronomy and mathematics shone brighter than all the gold they possessed.

But one of the highest points in history's long narrative, one that stands out, is an apex known as the "glory of Rome." A civilization that stretched far across the known world, bringing with it some of the most progressive advances: sanitation, intricate road systems, the 12-month calendar, aqueducts, the postal service, and enhancements to the legal system, the Romans made an indelible mark on society that has lasted well into the modern age. With a trained military that shook the borders far from the capital city, Rome was both feared and respected.

From humble beginnings as a small city and a handful of kings, the Senate was formed to usher in its Republican era, where rule followed a democratic form of government under consuls and tribunes. But with growth and conquest came increased responsibilities until the sheer size and political and economic demands paved the way for Augustus as its first recognized emperor. While the "glory of Rome" glows brightly during this period as an empire, rising to its lustrous apex as one of the greatest civilizations of all time, there are also dark shadows that are often overlooked.

Ultimate power, riches, and god-like status did not always rest well on men as they did on Augustus, Marcus Aurelius, and Constantine. These men assumed their duties as much for the state as for themselves, where both reveled in the glory of being Roman. They are remembered for their insight, vision, and courageous decisions more than their faults. But there were others, men who were unprepared for the demands of filling such a role, more concerned with their own desires or too caught up in venerating themselves to care about the greater good.

Dark smudges on the Roman banner, each of these emperors seemed to try and do their best to outdo any depravity and greed that had gone before them. Unwilling or unable to rise above ego and lust, they could not aspire to greatness, and so sunk to the depths of infamy. Nero's pyromaniac scandals, Domitian's fatal paranoia, and Elagabalus 'sexual experimentation set these men apart to strut through history in their own hall of shame.

This book unveils the immorality of regimental Rome. It delves into the very psyche of some flamboyant figures who paraded across the stage of one of history's most glorious eras with little regard for the stain they left behind in their wake. There are also those who fell far short of being great, making very impact at all while on the throne.

While certain parts might seem far-fetched or shamelessly like gossip from a trashy tabloid magazine, they are every bit fact. Each action is laid bare, all the flaws revealed to paint a picture of the worst leaders this great nation produced.

As a proud war veteran and ardent history teacher, August Mead's passion and insight into this period of ancient Rome will often startle you, mostly because it's all gobsmackingly true! With his crafty knack of storytelling based on in-depth research and extensive travels to many of the ruins where the events took place, he transports you back to the paved streets of the bustling city, the large halls of the revered Curia, and the grandeur of the inner courts of Palatine Hill.

Whether you're a history buff or an interested bystander, your curiosity will be rewarded as August Mead pulls back the curtains on thousands of years for you to absorb the sordid scandals of the day, feel the outrage of the citizens, and shake your head at the excessive demands of some of Rome's less than honorable emperors. Strap on your sandals, gird your garment around your waist, and join August Mead in one of the most shocking and entertaining exposés you will ever read about the Roman Empire.

Chapter 1:

The Role of an Emperor

Better a living beggar than a buried emperor.
—Jean de La Fontaine

The role of a leader is not just handed out to anyone. America's democracy rests on officials being nominated and then being voted in by the majority of the public. Despite its tenuous efforts at a similar political structure, Africa has seen its fair share of coup d'états that have resulted in military dictators ravishing the land. China, as a one-party government, leans not on public favor but on internal power to determine the next head of state.

But getting there is only half the job, and, regardless if a general forces his way into office, or an individual has the full support of the people, running a country is a completely different story. All the promises that were made need to be addressed and hopefully met. Foreign relations come into play and could determine allies or enemies. And, of course, the economy, one of the driving forces of a country, needs to be kept on track.

Even in ancient times, running a nation, especially an empire the size of Rome, came with its perks and its headaches, and not everyone was cut out for the job.

Path to the Top

Look at any government and you will see that, even though there is a framework that defines how leaders ascend to the top job, it's never always straightforward. Some presidents or dictators have manipulated or muscled their way to take center stage. The world has seen colorful characters come and go.

For Rome, it was no different. What started out as a republic, soon grew beyond its borders and extended outside of those who were managing its growth. The burden of running a vast empire needed more than a collective; it needed a strong hand and a fresh vision. After years of being governed by elected officials, power struggles resulted in chaos.

Julius Caesar was the answer. By setting himself up as overall ruler, he paved the path for a long line of emperors who would fill the top spot of reigning over one of the greatest nations. After his assassination, Octavian defeated Marc Antony and Cleopatra, enabling him to take full control and become Augustus, Rome's first emperor in 27 BCE (Magie, 1921).

Central to the governance and legacy of Rome, the emperor held immense political power and also defined the cultural and religious temperament of the people. Some wielded their authority with harsh cruelty, leaving a wake of corpses and fear behind them. Others abdicated all decisions of the government so they could indulge in hedonistic pleasure. Some took their office seriously enough to leave a legacy of wisdom and strength.

Not everyone who took the crown deserved to be there. Some, as this book will show, ruined the reputation of Rome, dragged every ounce of decency through the streets, and poured out the nation's wealth on their whims! So, how did such a person get to such a prominent position? What were the qualifications? While some followed legal and traditional pathways, others chose the route of usurpation, civil war, and military might.

With a growing empire and a political structure that was constantly adapting to the changes, being next in line to the throne was not always clear-cut or easy.

Legal and Traditional

Adoption was the preferred and recognized method for emperors to secure a successor. With no biological heir, emperors chose someone they thought would carry on their legacy in the best way possible. It was a very acceptable act that did not leave things to chance or a shaky bloodline. Augustus adopted Tiberius.

The other method was to gain the Senate's approval. Although it was not as powerful as it had been during the days of the Republic, its ceremonial importance held enough sway to back a candidate for the position of emperor. Even emperors who had assumed power through other ways looked to the Senate for endorsement as a way of legitimizing their office.

But even these methods were not always straightforward or ironclad. Personal ambition, political alliances, and the military's influence often came into play as well. Navigating the legal channels meant playing your cards right, scratching the necessary backs, and even marrying into the correct families.

Military Support

While Rome had significant political clout within the walls of the Senate halls, it also had one of the most formidable armies. The power that lay in the hands of generals was never to be underestimated, and, with the loyalty of his troops, a military leader could even challenge a ruling emperor.

If troops proclaimed their general as "*imperator*," they showed allegiance and endorsed his successes. It was enough for him to be able to march against whomever else stood in his way. Vespasian learned that legions in Egypt declared him emperor, catapulting him into a war against his opponent, and opening the path to the throne.

One of the strongest military powers, though, did not lie in the troops. The praetorian guard, the emperor's personal guard, wielded significant influence in and around the palace. On more than one occasion, they took matters into their own hands, assassinating emperors who had gone too far.

Sculpture of Roman War

Keeping the soldiers and guards happy was not an easy task, and while some emperors enjoyed their backing on the way up, if things turned, they would find themselves at the end of a sword by those same men.

Usurpation and Civil War

Sometimes a ruler just needed ambition and force to break down the doors to the palace. Despite the legal framework in place, seizing the throne through unlawful means was not beyond some individuals. Treachery and deceit sometimes spoke louder than traditional means, allowing people to get their foot in the door and wheedle their way in.

Wherever politics exist, corruption and bribery hide in the corners, as well as scheming and plotting. All through history, those with the right brand of propaganda have used it to their advantage. Elagabalus' grandmother's lie about bloodline is a case in point.

If manipulation did not work, then pure force often was the answer. Personal rivalries could spill over into the streets until two large factions were squaring up against each other for a chance at power. Civil war has always been the result of divided support, and Rome saw its fair share of these skirmishes.

Assassination

Since the day Julius Caesar stared back surprised at Brutus holding a bloody knife, one of the warnings for those in power was "watch your back!" Every brick of the Roman Palace was built with sweat, cement, and a dash of treachery. The shadows and corners of the imperial residence were always filled with whispers and plots.

Even if the legal or traditional methods were stacked in a person's favor, waiting in line could become tiresome. Sometimes getting to the throne meant removing the one who was in the way, regardless of whether he was your father, uncle, or a good ruler!

With so much power at stake, it is no surprise that 20% of all the emperors in Roman history were assassinated (Geggel, 2018). The rest cannot all be confirmed as normal ones with suspicious circumstances surrounding a few emperors coming to the throne after their brother or father suddenly passed away.

This was always a tricky method as it meant getting close to an already paranoid ruler who had the Praetorian Guard stationed close by as well as a few other safety measures in case someone turned on him. Tiberius lived in fear for his life, as did so many other emperors, which shows that even though it was not easy, it was more prevalent than rulers would have liked.

Divine Rights

While Rome revolved around politics and military campaigns, it was also deeply religious. Its pantheon of gods was central to every festival and every occurrence. Certain events, whether catastrophes or successes, were attributed to being ordained by spiritual forces.

Emperors often transcended the line between normal and spiritual. They were seen as god-like, having the divine right to rule. Augustus used this to great effect, claiming to be the "son of a god" to establish his place on the throne. This idea took hold and soon the custom of deifying dead emperors became common practice.

Claiming a connection to a divine lineage could bolster support and increase the chance of someone ascending to the role of leader. It was a fine line though, and one that some emperors, especially the infamous ones, often crossed, exalting themselves too early and too much!

Keeping Your Head

Once in power, it was not simply a position that allowed the emperor to enjoy himself to his full, although some took this route to their detriment. Appeasing the Senate, paying the soldiers good wages, and looking after the citizens were ways of ensuring approval from all the right places and people. While being a king, ruler, or emperor might sound like a dream job, the top spot comes with many demands, lots of ceremonies to follow, and plenty of decisions that can define or destroy his reign.

Job for Life

Unlike the consul, a role where a senator was elected to hold administrative authority over the city for a year, becoming an emperor had no expiry date, except when he died. There was no retirement or pension. Much like a king or monarch, the task of leading the nation could only pass to another person when he died.

For some rulers, this was great, as they enjoyed the support and admiration of their people, continuing to reign for many years until they passed away. But for others, who tested the patience of the Senate and the public, it was not ideal. Their actions riled the public into hatred and frustration until they wanted him gone. There was no voting the emperor out, and the only way to remove him was through murder, assassination, or suicide!

Absolute Power

The Senate no longer had all the authority, it was more a facade of administration for making things official. Once the Republic ended, real power shifted to the emperor. Although it was good to be endorsed by these politicians and listen to their demands and advice, any decisions of the leader could be made without their backing. In truth, the emperor was all-powerful, a dictator, and an autocrat.

This kind of dominance could be dangerous in the wrong hands, as it could be used for every whim and fancy of a lunatic or to quench the bloodlust of a sadist.

Legacy

Kings and rulers have always known that, even though they have all the power and money in the world, they do not have all the time they would like. For such important people, they consider it imperative that everybody knows who they are, and, after they die, who they were. There are many ways to leave a visible and lasting imprint of their once powerful and awesome lives on Earth.

Almost every emperor who served longer than a couple of years ended up remodeling Rome and building a palace to their liking. Sitting on the throne was not enough, powerful men always wanted to leave reminders for the citizens and future generations of who they were. From Egypt's pyramids to Babylon's hanging gardens, structures have been built in honor of these great people. If a statue was not enough, then they commanded artists make ones made of gold or ones that towered far above all the others.

Another way of lasting beyond a reign was through lineage. Setting up a dynasty ensured your name passed from generation to generation. It did depend heavily on having a son capable of taking over.

Statue of woman and child

A much more difficult legacy was the manner in which an emperor ruled. Marcus Aurelius is remembered for being wise and philosophical, while Trajan was a highly skilled military leader, and Hadrian's intellect and architectural pursuits gained him fame. Of course, the aftermath of some rulers that are listed in this book left nothing but scandal and infamy smeared across their names.

Wives

Having a wife was important, not only because having an heir to take the throne ensured an emperor's legacy, but it could also consolidate political power. Marrying into the right family or social group has always been used by rulers to support and strengthen their crown. Often a marriage was more out of convenience than for love, and this did not always bring happiness to the palace.

Some wives could wield as much power as their husbands. This could bolster the emperor's standing or cause chaos and conspiracy, depending on the woman's motives once she made it into the palace.

Luxury and Wealth

Along with the job, came the perks. The palace, the amenities, and all the money of the nation. Although the Senate was supposed to oversee administration and finance, the emperor could use whatever he wanted for whatever he desired. Augustus was the richest of the lot and is estimated in today's currency to have been worth $4.6 trillion (Hallman, 2019).

This could be used on military campaigns, building projects, or even outlandish banquets. It depended on what type of emperor was in office, and what his vision for the empire was. A few have gone down in history as almost bankrupting Rome because of their lavish tastes and ridiculous appetites.

Public Support

Rome was the Senate, the Republic, an emperor, palaces, and the might of the army. But Rome was also the masses. Thousands of people made up a significant base of power that, if used properly, could propel a person to great heights. It could also bring an emperor down if the mob was not kept happy.

When it came to the general public, a policy of "bread and circuses" was often part of an emperor's reign. Handing out free grain or food staved the hunger, keeping riots at bay. Gladiator games and chariot races were always good ways of distracting the cheering crowds from any glaring political problems.

While the power of the people had diminished with the passing of the Republic, ignoring the citizens was something an emperor always did at their own risk and peril.

Chapter 2:

Nero's Reign of Excess

An emperor's an entertainer, an empire a supershow.
—Nero

Flames furiously spit and lick the night, close enough that he can feel the heat on his face as he stares out across the city. This is not a fire to huddle around, warming your hands. Every building and structure is engulfed, smoke billowing up, blackening an already gloomy sky. There are screams below, people running and shouting as they flee the scorching blaze or try and save their possessions.

He does not flee. He slouches, robes open as his rotund body sweats against the steaming air. He does not scream. He strums on his cithara, singing to the crackling rhythm of the inferno. His is a song of indifference, of casual pleasure in watching the purge of a city. The beady eyes do not see destruction or citizens in pain, only the majestic future he will build in its place.

He stops playing his song to wipe the sweat from his brow with a thick hand. A smile creeps onto his face. This fire is not just the rise of his greatness, but it will be the downfall of a people that have been a thorn in his side for too long.

This is the picture history has painted of the empire's fifth ruler. This is the portrayal of Nero, the image of a madman, a heartless dictator fiddling while all of Rome burns. Whether he received a bad rap from jealous writers and was the focus of their propaganda or he really was that nasty is still a fierce debate between historians. But, in the end, there is no denying the untimely deaths that surrounded him, the fire that gutted Rome, and the absurd actions he took during his reign. They could all be the conjuring of a demented mind or the results of an overbearing, controlling mother.

Mother Issues

Lucius Domitius Ahenobarbus was born on 15 December, 37 CE in the coastal village of Antium, the son of a former Roman consul (Jarus, 2013). This would have been enough to give him a step in the right direction: being born as a freedman with some sort of status. But it was his mother's side of the family that would ultimately dictate the young boy's passage toward the throne.

Agrippina the Younger was related to power and royalty. Her great-uncle was the famed Tiberius, who assumed the title of emperor once Augustus, her great-grandfather, died. Next, her brother, Caligula, took the mantle and reigned over Rome. Through her bloodline, she was inextricably linked to Palatine Hill, the emperor's household. The benefits of having such a powerful family meant everything of the best was available to her and her son, Lucius, which was especially handy when her husband died.

Agrippina the Younger

Living in the emperor's house had its upsides; however, sharing close quarters with an incestuous madman like Caligula saw Agrippina and her cousin finally hatch a plan to oust the unruly sibling. Not much is known of the *Plot of the Three Daggers*, but, as assassination attempts went, it was nothing new or strange, with four out of twelve rulers meeting their end this way (Wasson, 2018). Somehow, Caligula got wind of what his sister and cousin had planned, and it backfired, resulting in Agrippina being banished to the Pontine Islands.

Lucius, only 3 years old at the time, was left in the care of his aunt and had to wait another two years before Caligula was finally murdered. As fate would have it, Claudius (Agrippina's uncle) was discovered hiding behind a curtain the moment the knife blades ended Caligula's life. Unwilling and reluctant, Claudius found himself thrust into the role of ruler. One of the new emperor's acts was to lift the exile so that Lucius could be reunited with his mother, Agrippina. Little did Claudius know, but he had signed his own demise by accepting them back into his household.

Agrippina's Schemes

The ever-ambitious woman now turned her sights on greater aspirations for her son, pulling strings to ensure Lucius had more than a spitting chance of being crowned. But her first obstacle was none other than Cladius 'wife, Messalina, who decided she would need to do something to protect her own son's chances at becoming emperor. According to Suetonius (Hansley, 2018), she sent assassins into Lucius ' bedroom to finish him off, but instead, they fled the scene after seeing a coiled snake guarding the boy. However, there was no serpent, only its skin, and, as an act of defiance or a symbol of good luck, Agrippina had it gilded into a bracelet for her son.

The women's feud reached a climax until Agrippina spread word of an affair Messalina was having behind Claudius 'back, and the emperor had his wife executed. With a space open next to the most powerful man in the realm, Agrippina quickly stepped in, filling the spot. The next step was to have Lucius implanted as a contender for succession, which his mother achieved by convincing her new husband to adopt the young boy. It was at this point in 49 CE that he underwent a change of name, thanks to his mother, and he officially became known as Nero (Jarus, 2013)!

But Agrippina was not finished, and there was one more play to seal the deal involving Claudius 'daughter, Octavia. Having already removed her fiancé from the picture after spreading rumors of an affair, Nero married his stepsister at the age of fifteen, which meant he would then be the heir apparent (Mead, 2021). But with his mother always in the picture, any chance of the marriage of convenience working out was doomed from the start.

The close oedipal relationship Nero shared with Agrippina has even been stretched by certain accounts to include a deep, depraved form of incest, as she apparently "presented herself attractively attired to her half-intoxicated son and offered him her person" (Mead, 2021). Added to this are the stories of a mistress Nero had who bore a striking resemblance to his own mother (Levine, 2020). This alone would have set him up to be one of the more licentious rulers, a target for gossip among the citizens. Whatever the nature of the connection, Agrippina's influence was firmly grasping for imperial status.

Not content that her teenage son was waiting in line for the throne, Agrippina's motivation could not wait for Claudius to make way for Nero. Whether the old man ate a bad mushroom that disagreed with his internal system, or it was laced with something to intensify the attack on his stomach, the emperor finally succumbed to the succession plot his wife had been planning for so long.

Taking Control

At the age of 17, Nero, not Claudius 'own son, Britannicus, was crowned ruler of Rome. As if to cement her role in Nero's elevation, Agrippina's face was depicted on official coins along with her son's, as well as a statue made to commemorate the coronation of her placing a crown on his head (Mead, 2021). These unprecedented moves reveal how ingrained she was in political maneuvers and making decisions for Nero.

The next move was an obvious one, considering there was still a legitimate heir to the throne in the midst, roaming the corridors of power. Claudius' real son surely should have seen a pattern emerging. It was no surprise then, that soon after losing his rightful place on the throne, Britannicus died—another obstacle removed.

The way forward seemed open for Nero to do as he pleased, except that he was still answerable to his advisers, one of whom was Agrippina. However, two years into his reign, he had had enough of her meddling. Suddenly, her face no longer graced any Roman coins after 55 CE, and she was not consulted anymore on state matters, which fell entirely to Seneca, Nero's long-time tutor, and Burrus, the commander of the Praetorian Guard (Jarus, 2013). After working in tandem for so long to reach a goal, they both realized only one person was left who blocked their path to greatness—each other! The drastic decision to kill his mother off may have been a response to her plotting to get rid of him, since she had been warned by an astrologer shortly after Nero's birth of dying by her own son's hand (Jarus, 2013).

Rather than trust his Praetorian Guard with the duty, an elaborate plan of sinking a boat she would travel on was concocted, although this failed. Agrippina had worked too hard and long to be denied her rightful place, and she swam to safety. But Nero was enjoying his moment of glory far too much to allow her to ruin it for him, and, in the end, assassins were dispatched to finish the job.

While killing your mother was usually a terrible crime in ancient Rome, the death of Agrippina was applauded by some. Not only was Nero congratulated by the senators, but it marked a turning point in his time as emperor. Without his mother, he was his own man and began making his own decisions to rule and to live as he pleased!

Nero did not stop with only killing his mother, and, soon after, when he became tired of Octavia, he had her put to death, too. He had previously tried by strangling her, then he divorced her because she could not give him a child, and, when this did not go down well with everyone, he bribed someone to confess to an adulterous affair with her so she could be executed (Jarus, 2013). His second wife, Poppea, managed to become pregnant, but, despite being madly in love with her, Nero kicked her in the stomach, causing her to die after she had complained about him returning late from the races. Claudius' daughter, Antonia, refused to marry Nero and met her end.

Sex and Excess

As emperor, Nero seemed to start off well. Perhaps it was having Seneca, Burrus, and his mother to guide him that steered him in diplomatic avenues. Many of the reforms he brought were good enough to remain in law, being kept and built on by later rulers. Some of them, however, may have frustrated the wealthy since they aimed at giving back to the commoners. But they were still lauded by many as good, winning him popularity with the crowds. As Hareth Al Bustani (Jarus, 2013) writes:

> Nero promised to uproot the corruption that plagued Claudius ' court and return powers to the Senate... Nero actually stuck to his words... The emperor was a man who appealed to all classes alike—he handed 400 sesterces to every citizen, gave the Praetorians free grain, greeted soldiers by name, introduced a salary for impoverished senators, built a beautiful new market, scored military victories abroad, held the most spectacular games Rome had ever seen, and tackled predatory tax farming practices. (para. 8-9)

Rebecca Mead (2021) mentions similar feats approved by the greater public:

> He erected a spectacular complex of public baths, which allowed ordinary citizens to indulge ablutionary pleasures previously reserved for the wealthy. At the end of the first century, the satirical poet Martial quipped, "Who was ever worse than Nero? Yet what can be better than Nero's warm baths?" (para. 15)

While he may have had a hand in certain economic improvements, social transformations, and keeping the empire from completely crumbling, being a wealthy totalitarian (and having no mother to scold him) gave him license to do as he pleased. It was as though the lid had been lifted on a young man bursting to entertain himself.

Emperor Nero

For sexual thrills, he re-enacted weddings with some of his favorite freedmen, consummating the fake nuptials for all to witness, as well as skulking around at night in disguise to do as he pleased with women and boys (Mead, 2021). One such boy was named Sporus, whom Nero castrated so he would be more of a woman that Nero could marry and have as a wife. Seutonius (Hays, 2018) writes about his love for raucous parties when he says:

Little by little, however, as his vices grew stronger, he dropped jesting and secrecy and with no attempt at disguise openly broke out into worse crime. He prolonged his revels from midday to midnight, often livening himself by a warm plunge, or, if it were summer, into water cooled with snow. Sometimes, too, he closed the inlets and banqueted in public in the great tank in the Campus Martius, or in the Circus Maximus, waited on by harlots and dancing girls from all over the city. (para. 27)

If the claims of his lurid behavior are to be believed, then he was game for anything and everything. Even if some of it was part of a smear campaign or simply gossip, there's enough of it to believe that many of the stories were indeed true.

Dying to Be Heard

But his greatest passion lay in the halls of art, the theater of song, and the arena of sport. Against the advice of Seneca and Burrus, and with his mother gone, he practiced his talents in public, reciting poems, singing songs, and taking part in races.

Although he did not have the greatest voice, this did not deter him from following his dream of learning the cithara (a type of lyre or harp) and taking singing lessons. His serious approach meant listening to Terpnus, the best lyre player, as well as taking on a strict regimen of lying down with a heavy lead plate on his chest, vomiting all the excess food out, and staying away from anything that could injure his voice (Hays, 2018). Despite all his best efforts and long-winded performances, Nero remained a mediocre entertainer.

To ensure he had a rapt audience, no one was permitted to leave while he was singing, even if it was urgent. With the gates locked, women in labor had to give birth during performances, others leaped from the high walls, and even some pretended to be dead so they would be carried out (Hays, 2018). Nero always had a full house, regardless of how good or bad he was. Not one to pass up an opportunity to take the stage, the emperor popped up in numerous public performances, sometimes with a mask on, often without.

He was not deterred, and, as a lover of the Greek theater, he traveled across to Greece with a large entourage to compete in several of the festivals there. His presentations earned him 1,808 first-place prizes, and, if that was not enough, the Olympic officials added singing and acting to the contest just so the emperor could strut his stuff for the audience (Jarus, 2013). When he returned to Rome, he hardly ever spoke to anyone directly, using an elocutionist to deliver any messages so he could save his voice for singing.

A Need for Speed

When he wasn't hogging the limelight from other actors and singers, Nero could be found at the chariot races. As a young boy, he dreamed and talked about the horses at the circus, even though his tutors forbade him from doing so. His passion grew stronger, and, in his early days as emperor, he was often playing with ivory chariots on a board. At every opportunity, he would sneak out in disguise to watch any race that was taking place. Later, he ditched the secrecy, until it became known that when a chariot race was taking place in Rome, Nero was sure to be watching (Hays, 2018).

The drive to be holding the reigns, feeling the precarious speed of the wheels turning corners in the dust as the horses charged ahead became too strong for Nero to ignore any longer. It wasn't long before he was practicing in his gardens in front of the slaves until he finally made an appearance at the Circus Maximus. But he was not content, craving the reputation of racing at the greatest sporting event, and so he made his way to Greece to take part in the Olympics.

Just like his singing, Nero did not have to worry about whether he was good or bad at something, as long as he won. In one dangerous race, the chariot lifted, throwing him from the car. Sprawled in the dust, humiliated at the accident, Nero angrily got up and dusted himself off only to find that even though he had not been able to finish, he was still awarded the wreath of victory (Jarus, 2013). For this, the judges received a reward of one million sesterces.

Chariot racing in the Colosseum

If he was not racing, Nero used a chariot to make grand entrances, whether in Antium or Albanum. When he entered Rome, he went all out: being pulled by white horses, he rode in the same car that Augustus had used when triumphant and wore a purple robe and Greek cloak of gold stars with his Olympic crown on his head as perfume was sprinkled ahead, birds were released, and ribbons were showered upon him (Hays, 2018).

Costly Extravagance

Access to unlimited power and money at the same time can lead to devastating consequences if it's in the wrong hands. After he got rid of his mother, Nero decided he no longer needed the dry, regimented advice of Seneca and Burrus. He swapped them out for someone who would appreciate his lewd fascinations: Tigellinus, a member of Caligula's household, was appointed in the role. Rather than curb the emperor's behavior, he encouraged it.

For Nero, while the coffers were full, there was a good time to be had. Not just any type of pleasure, but the wildest, most lavish that money could buy. Economics bored him, and keeping track of his spending seemed like a waste of time when he could be having fun. In his own words: "There is no other way of enjoying riches and money than by riotous extravagance, declaring that only stingy and niggardly fellows kept a correct account of what they spent" (Jasiński, n.d.-b).

As stylish dressers went, he was known for never wearing the same outfit twice. He gave presents without any thought of the cost and only went on journeys with a minimum of 1,000 carriages, the horses' hooves shod with silver (Hays, 2018). Nero enjoyed gambling and played dice often, spending up to four hundred thousand sesterces on a single point.

However, his ultimate expense came in the form of architecture.

Once the Great Fire had ravaged most of Rome, razing it to the ground, Nero could finally build his dream palace. Whether it had always been his intention to flatten everything so he could rebuild what he wanted or not, the end result was far beyond anything ever erected before. It was to trounce his previous renovations that had begun linking all the existing residences into a large one with extensive gardens.

While building projects were a normal part of an emperor's reign, allowing them to model and put their unique stamp on the city they ruled, Nero's Golden Palace was larger and more complex than anything that had been erected before or after.

The vision was to stretch from Palatine Hill down to Esquiline Hill, an area of around 50 hectares with 300 rooms, pristine gardens, a bath complex only for the emperor, and even an artificial lake for a ship to sail on (Mingoia, 2023). No expense was spared, sinking a massive part of Rome's economy and grabbing any funding he could get his hands on into this egotistical venture.

Rooms included an octagonal structure culminating in a dome that allowed the light in through an oculus (a hole in the top). He built the Nymphaeum, which resembled a seaside cave complete with cascading water and seashell-lined walls, and a rotating dining room that moved around via water mechanisms. Walls were either clad in marble or covered in extensive frescoes. Probably the most narcissistic was the 120-foot planned golden statue of himself.

At the time of Nero's death, the palace had not been finished, and much of it would be destroyed soon after that.

The Burning Issue

Nero's travels to Greece, his flagrant disregard for dealing with outlying rebellions, and his excessive lifestyle were coming to a head. Instead of rushing back to deal with matters, he took his time to enlighten others about the virtues of music. Without Seneca and Burrus at his side, governance seems to have slipped to a degree that began worrying the people. The similarities to Caligula's reign made the Senate and the public edgy, and a nagging criticism from a small devout group made it harder for him to do as he pleased.

There are conflicting stories as to how involved Nero was, and whether he was to blame at all. But he was extremely quick to point the finger and even quicker at using the opportunity to begin his construction of the Golden Palace. The timing seems too convenient, almost like a typical cover-up campaign to distract the public from real political problems.

It was a balmy mid-summer night with hot winds blowing across the city. Shops had closed, and the Circus Maximus was empty. July 18th 64 CE was like any other night, except for the spark that set the night alight. Beginning near the Circus, it jumped quickly across the narrow, winding streets, engulfing stores and sweeping across the level areas. Soon the flames were racing up the hills toward the imperial residence where they burned brightly before turning to rush into the valley again, raging back and forth for 10 days (Mingoia, 2023).

People grabbed what they could and headed to the country roads, the only place they could find safety from the fire. From there they could only watch helplessly as everything they owned went up in flames.

Some reports indicate that they may have been prevented from trying to put the fire out, and certain witnesses claim men were acting under orders when they threw burning logs into the city (Hays, 2018). Most legitimate records also put the emperor himself 30 miles from the scene of the crime at Antium, the place of his birth.

His response was noteworthy, rushing back to provide aid and food to those who needed it, opening his gardens for the homeless, and initiating reconstruction. But, just like the fire, rumors and resentment had already gained traction, rushing through the province like wildfire. News of plans for a newer, grander Golden Palace only stoked these embers.

Nero, however, had one more play left to hold onto his dwindling popularity and turned the blame onto the Christians, a small sect in the city at that time. Nero seemed to take extra delight in this new crackdown on the "guilty" party, going to extreme lengths to find innovative ways to execute them. Always one for public entertainment, he ordered any of the members of the religious group to be killed either by dressing them in animal skins and letting dogs feast on them, being nailed to crosses as live bait in the arenas, or as human torches to light the way at night (Jarus, 2013).

Reading one of Paul, the apostle's, letters to the Christians, the persecution they faced daily can be felt in his words:

> We are pressed on every side by troubles, but we are not crushed. We are perplexed, but not driven to despair. We are hunted down, but never abandoned by God. We get knocked down, but we are not destroyed. Through suffering, our bodies continue to share in the death of Jesus so that the life of Jesus may also be seen in our bodies. Yes, we live under constant danger of death because we serve Jesus, so that the life of Jesus will be evident in our dying bodies. (NLT Bible, 2017, 2 Cor. 8-11 NLT)

Both Paul and Peter, two of Christianity's most prominent leaders, met their ends by being beheaded and crucified upside down, respectively. While this may have momentarily distracted many, it could not stop Nero's publicity ratings from dropping to an all-time low.

No Way Back

With taxes up, people were grumbling. Nero had his fingers in everyone's pockets, even the temples as he scraped together any gold or silver to fund his building project. And all the while, he continued his extravagant lifestyle. The whispers of dissension were getting louder.

A plot to remove the emperor and have him replaced by another senator was uncovered. One of the conspirators, tribune Subrius Flavus, explained his reasons when he said, "I began to hate you when you turned into the murderer of your mother and wife—a chariot-driver, an actor, a fire-raiser" (Jarus, 2013). Tigellinus, Nero's close advisor, was tasked with rooting out those involved. Instead, he targeted anyone who was thought to be against the emperor. Even Seneca, Nero's long-time tutor and counsel in his early days, found himself in Tigellinus' crosshairs and was forced to commit suicide.

But wiping out his enemies did not stop the rot, and, by 68 CE, there were more voices crying out against the ruler, much louder and more public this time. Gaius Iulius Vindex, a governor in Gaul, renounced Nero and put his support behind another senator (Jarus, 2013). The uprising was quelled, but not before the rallying cry had been picked up and carried across the nation. The next in line to reject the leadership of Nero was none other than his own Praetorian Guard, those tasked with guarding him.

Now an enemy of the state, there was no way back for him. On June 9, Nero, always the number one entertainer in his own eyes, cried "What an artist dies in me!" before ending his own life (Jarus, 2013).

Running For His Life

Faced with expulsion, Nero could not decide what to do. The humiliation of pleading and publicly apologizing for all he had done was too much for him to admit. It would have meant throwing himself at the mercy of his nominated successor, Galba. He even contemplated seeking out refuge from the Parthians, Rome's enemies. But, in the end, Nero opted to take no immediate action, and he went to bed.

In the middle of the night, he woke up to find the palace deserted. Sensing something was up, Nero fled the palace, riding on his horse to one of his ex-slave's villas. Phaon had been sympathetic to the emperor, and possibly even held some sort of office during his reign (Meddings, 2022). On being recognized by a soldier along the way, Nero veered off on a detour, where he fumbled and struggled through bushes and brambles to get to his destination.

When he finally arrived scratched, tired, and frantic, he received news that the Senate had declared him an enemy of the state. Realizing he had no way to reclaim his throne or find anyone else who would have pity on him, Nero contemplated suicide. But it was something he could not do, and he asked those in the villa to demonstrate. No one could help him in this regard, leaving Nero to fret in indecision.

His paranoia had reached such a fevered state that, mistaking the noises he heard outside for those of horses bearing guards to come and arrest him, the ex-emperor grabbed a dagger and drove it into his throat. Devoid of any of the ceremonies he had become used to, with no applauding audience he had craved, hiding in an outlying house far from his unfinished palace, Nero died.

Chaos and Rumor

The sudden vacuum caused by Nero's end resulted in chaos. A number of emperors filled the gap for a short time each, none of them able to bring any kind of order to Rome. Many people, still loyal to their chariot-racing, singing leader, swore he was still alive, and rumors and impostors kept popping up all over the empire for a long time after his death.

This dogged support shows that either his carefree ways were popular with the masses or many of the sordid stories written about him may not hold as much water as many have been led to believe. Some, like the Christians, saw Nero as the antichrist, a person who ruled as immorally as possible. Others claimed he was a breath of fresh air who spoke to the common man, breaking hierarchical stereotypes. There are even those who maintain he had a vision to modernize the city, even if it was wrapped up in his own ego. But, if most of the anecdotes are to be believed, then he is that madman, who lived as excessively and uncaringly as he could.

Most of Nero's Golden Palace was torn down, the artificial lake and baths filled in, and any other reminder of his reign removed as a warning to anyone of what can happen when power and money are allowed unchecked in the hands of a megalomaniac.

Chapter 3:

Caligula's Mad Desires

Would that the Roman people had but one neck!
–Caligula

Eighteen servants scurried around the marble room, making sure Incitatus had everything he desired. The ivory container had been filled with gold-flecked oats fit for a king. The purple outfit that boasted royalty had been scrubbed clean, and the jewel-encrusted choker that went around his neck was polished to a bright sheen, all ready for him to wear for his guests. Dignitaries were on the way to dine with this head of state, and everything had to be perfect for such a prominent figure.

For any normal consul of Rome, this may have been acceptable privileges, except that Incitatus was actually a horse! Caligula, the third emperor, was certainly crazy, mad enough to pull off a stunt as insane as proclaiming his favorite animal as the leader of the Senate. An unstable combination of power, paranoia, and pride resulted in a reign that became all about him, even to the point of believing he was a god to be worshiped.

Insane or just callous, Caligula's antics have become legendary, but all for the wrong reasons!

A Popular Choice

In the same coastal village of Antium that produced the nefarious Nero, Caligula was born on 31 August, 12 CE to Germanicus, a popular war hero, and Agrippina the Elder (Bileta, 2020). Although he was given the name of Gaius Julius Cesar, a tribute to his imperial dynasty, he also picked up the nickname of Caligula. Traveling with his father to the Rhine frontier, he became a favorite with the legionaries there, who dressed him up in a little soldier's uniform. The small boots, called *caligae*, are likely where this moniker came from. Wherever he went, he was welcomed with open arms, except in the Roman palace.

Even though he held a prominent place in Roman society because of his name and bloodline, and even though he was well-liked because of who his father was, he had also inherited a target on his back. A paranoid Tiberius, the emperor at the time, suspected many plots from the Senate against him, and anyone he thought might be eyeing the top spot. Whether by his own hand or that of Sejanus, his administrator, those who presented a threat to the throne were killed.

Caligula was seven years old when he accompanied his parents to the East. There his father got malaria and died, although there were whispers that it was poison that finished him off and not disease! Caligula and his mother returned to Rome, where the atmosphere was thick with plots. Tiberius was strangely absent when Rome gathered to welcome the ashes of the fallen hero, and, soon, Agrippina and her family were added to Sejanus' list of threats to the emperor. They were first banished, but it wasn't long before Agrippina and her other two sons were executed. It seems even Tiberius had a soft spot for Caligula, as he was miraculously spared from the purge since there was no proper heir to the throne.

For six years, Caligula was watched and monitored, almost as a hostage in the imperial palace as he was groomed to take over one day. At times, he would stay on the island of Capri where Tiberius had a heavily guarded villa. With little freedom, and always under lock and key, Caligula could do nothing until the day his great-uncle died. What he did very well though, was smile in the presence of his enemies. There is speculation that he may have thought and even half-attempted to murder the old man, but any ill feelings he had toward him were kept under wraps.

Instead, he found favor with Tiberius and was afforded political positions within the government, giving him a very good chance to win over more allies. His likable nature and ability to play the part proved to be enough to keep him alive as well as set him up to take over from his great-uncle.

A Fresh Start

When Tiberius eventually died of natural causes (although there were also rumors of a pillow and suffocation) Rome woke up to a new reign. Overnight on 17th March 37 CE, a new emperor was ushered onto the scene. There was another prospect in Gemellus, but he was sidelined mainly because of the public endorsement Caligula received from Macro, a prefect in charge of the Praetorian Guard (Bileta, 2020). Despite the years of being trapped in the same house as the man who killed his family, Caligula did not immediately unleash any pent-up anger and revenge. Instead, he was welcomed by the public and Senate with open arms, and, in turn, he responded with charisma and energy. Incredibly popular as his father had been, it seemed that the days of treasonous paranoia were behind the Roman courts.

Perhaps it was having a level-headed adviser, but the reforms Caligula brought about were met with great support from all of Rome. Tiberius' notorious trials to weed out traitors came to an end, many were allowed to return from exile, and all the records Sejanus had kept were burned. On the economic front, unfair taxes were done away with, and he rewarded the public with a great show of gladiatorial games and chariot races (Bileta, 2020). It seemed he could do no wrong, and that the political tides had turned.

When it came to construction, Caligula set about making sure certain buildings that Tiberius had started were completed. New projects of extending the aqueducts and building a new amphitheater in Pompeii began in earnest, as well as an extension of the port to handle more grain from Egypt. His sweeping changes were like a breath of fresh air to the stale, secretive days of Tiberius, and it's why he was admired by everyone in "all the world, from the rising to the setting sun" (Bileta, 2020).

Bust of Caligula

But the days of sunshine did not last, and a turning point in Caligula's reign revealed a completely different and much darker side of the popular young ruler during the rest of his days.

A Sudden Shift

At the age of 25, not long after taking the throne, Caligula fell ill. It was serious enough to see him out of action for a number of months while all of Rome prayed for his health. Whether it was a nervous breakdown, severe epilepsy, or some other disease has never been accurately proved, but his generous and diplomatic demeanor seems to have been stolen from him by whatever happened.

The sickness not only robbed him of his sanity, but some reports say he was not completely healthy in his body either. According to Sandison (1958), Caligula had various physical side effects:

> His head was bald but his body hirsute. He was sound neither in body nor mind: as a boy he was troubled with the 'falling sickness'. In youth he was at times unable to walk, stand up, collect his thoughts and to hold up his head. He was tormented by insomnia, never sleeping more than three hours at a time and experiencing vivid dreams. To this weakness there was added, paradoxically, extreme assurance but excessive timorousness so that he was afraid of thunder or lightning and even of the smoke from the crater of Mount Etna. (para. 42)

Whatever it was, when he eventually left his sick bed, the popular boy emperor had become a vengeful, sadistic young man. Caligula's remaining days would be filled with bizarre behavior, cruelty, and the belief that he was more than just a man.

A Darker Side

Although the Republic was capable of managing and administrating in his absence, there may also have been plots and schemes to remove the young emperor while he lay on his bed. It may explain why one of his first acts when he recovered was to come out swinging at any opponents. Macro, his supporter in the Praetorian Guard, had become less enamored with the way things were going, and any words he said against Caligula were taken as treason. He was executed, and Gemellus,

Caligula's previous rival for the throne, was forced to commit suicide. It was just the start.

Caligula began to distance himself from anyone who was a threat, allowing only those who would do his bidding or go along with his ideas to be near him. This behavior was very reminiscent of Tiberius' last days! Caligula would go on to have countless other people murdered and killed, often in the most savage ways he could imagine, like being sawed in two or being fed to beasts (Sandison, 1958). He needed almost no excuse to order a decapitation, and simply by nodding his head in a person's direction, they would be killed on the spot.

He enjoyed watching the pain and agony of those being tortured and even encouraged his executioners to take it slow by telling them, "Make him feel that he is dying" (Aldrete, 2019). During a religious ceremony, instead of smashing the bull's head with a hammer, he used the tool on the priest's assistant who was holding the animal.

Not all of his torturous games were fatal, and some were simply to make people suffer unnecessarily. From making senators run alongside his chariot in their togas to removing the shade at public entertainments during the heat of midday, he reveled in seeing others' pain and humiliation. If he came across a man who had a good head of hair, he would stop and order it to be shaved off, probably because Caligula himself was balding (Aldrete, 2019).

Morally Bankrupt

Although his brothers had been killed, Caligula's three sisters survived the purge and lived closely with him in the palace after Tiberius had died. This extremely close relationship with the young emperor has always been questionable, with some claiming depraved sexual misconduct. According to Suetonius (Aldrete, 2019), even though he enjoyed sex with all of them in front of guests, his favorite was Drusilla, whom he named as heir to the throne and, when she died, called her a goddess. If he was not guilty of incest, then he was known for raping a senator's wife or other lewd acts of brazen sexual depravity that he became known for.

He was often seen in women's clothing, so homosexuality was apparently not out of the question, as certain accounts claim he had affairs with Mnester, Marcus Lepidus, and Valerius Catullus (Sandison, 1958). Orgies were not uncommon, involving every type of sexual fantasy and licentious behavior possible. When he ran out of money, his way of funding his many lustful hobbies was to open part of the palace as a brothel with servants and boys for hire. All of this carried on despite Caligula being married to Caesonia, a beautiful woman whom he paraded nude for his subjects.

Not content with these sexual depravities, Caligula stripped back the curtains of his room as he lay naked and invited the Moon to come into his bed! His idea that he was some kind of god allowed him to think that he operated on a level above normal humans.

Lavish Lunacy

Tiberius' huge fortune he had gathered so meticulously was completely emptied on every whim and fancy in just two years of Caligula's reign. The only person who was amazed and even envious of such a feat was Nero! For the rest of Rome at that time, the unrestrained spending and extravagance resulted in higher taxes, new levies, and more property being seized to pay for it all. Chariot races, wasteful parties, fruitless campaigns, and an excessive lifestyle drained the economy.

In an attempt to be a military hero, Caligula marched the entire army out toward Gaul and Germany, but nothing was accomplished: no grand victory, just a waste of time and money! Then, he announced that he was invading Britain, but, instead, all the soldiers were lined up along the sandy beaches of the English Channel and ordered to collect seashells, the spoils of war (Aldrete, 2019). Failing to invade Britain, Caligula declared war on the sea itself, making his men whip the waves! As far-fetched as these stories sound, they have become the legacy of an emperor renowned for the bizarre.

Captivated by water, Caligula is reported to have ordered a few ships that would be floating palaces where he and his sexual partners could while away the day on Lake Nemi. The expense of such undertakings and their extravagant designs underlies the emperor's obsession with hedonism. Suetonius (Meddings, 2020) describes these outlandish orgy vessels:

> He had constructed some Liburnian galleys, their prows studded with jewels, their sails of many colours, whose ample interiors housed baths, porticoes, and dining-rooms as well as a large variety of vines and fruit-trees, so that lounging on these vessels he might travel by day along the shores of Campania entertained by choirs and orchestras. (para. 4)

Benito Mussolini (a later dictator who was transfixed with the glory of Rome) spent exorbitant amounts of money to drain the lake and bring the artifacts up for preservation in a museum in 1929 and 1931 (Meddings, 2020). But they were ruined by malicious fire at the hands of soldiers under another tyrant: Hitler.

In another indulgent attempt at glory, the emperor ordered a three-mile-long temporary bridge made of merchant ships to be constructed across the Bay of Naples in 39 C.E. so that the army could march back and forth, and he could ride his horse, Incitatus, "across" the water (Aldrete, 2019). As magnificent as replicating what Xerxes had done many years before was, it had a detrimental effect of adding to an already devastating famine back in Rome because of all the grain ships he used in his construction. The seemingly pointless exercise may have shown how much wealth and power he had, but the impact was far more damaging.

A Living God

It was not strange for certain rulers to be praised as though they were gods. The Egyptians had been doing it for years: Xerxes had been venerated by the Persians, and even Alexander the Great was deified. But in Rome, where logic, republic, and order formed the backbone of society, declaring someone to be god while they were still alive and setting up images to be worshiped was possibly a step too far. It was only done when an emperor died, elevating him to the status of divinity. Caligula, however, did not think this should be the case.

Reports indicate that he would often dress up like Venus or Jupiter, strutting around in a purple robe, thinking he was divine and often was seen "talking" with the gods (Aldrete, 2019). It may have been a result of the illness in his brain or unlimited power and money went to his head, but Caligula began to assert himself as a living god. In Rome, the people were still reluctant to buy into such a concept.

After his illness, he became frustrated with the Senate and its efforts to curtail his spending or outrageous acts. He constantly fought with them, enjoyed humiliating certain senators and tribunes, and even threatened to name his horse as consul! Things deteriorated quickly when the treason trials he had abolished in his first days as emperor were suddenly reintroduced. This cultivated an air of suspicion and paranoia, similar to his predecessor!

But the height of tension came when he demanded that they build him his own temple and declare him a deity. He began replacing the heads of some statues with his own and ordered his face to be on coins. It was Caligula here, there, and everywhere! If that did not rile up the Senate, then trying to move the capital city to Alexandria, Egypt where they would worship him as the god he was, proved to alienate him from almost every member of the governing body.

Coins with Emperors Faces

Having the Senate as an enemy was dangerous, but Caligula set about infuriating another group of zealous people, as well, with his ideas of being a god. Massive unrest swept through the Jews after he proposed they erect a statue of himself in the Temple of Jerusalem (Sandison, 1958). This was another headache for the administrators and senators of Rome to have to deal with, and, for some, it proved to be one step too many for their beloved nation.

An Abrupt End

The volatile atmosphere saw a number of plots and plans to dethrone the emperor, even from his own brother-in-law. His sister, Agrippina the Younger, was accused of treason and banished after a failed attempt to wrestle power back from the madman. Thousands more met a worse fate simply because Caligula suspected they had their eyes on his throne. A reign of terror gripped Rome that was worse than during Tiberius' days.

Cassius Chaerea, a tribune Caligula had taken great delight in humiliating in front of the rest of the Senate, secured the backing of the Praetorian Guard, the imperial security detail tasked with protecting the emperor. A plan was in motion to end the reign of tyranny and madness.

On January 24th, 41 CE, Caligula was enjoying the Palatine Games, watching a performance at the theater after having sacrificed a flamingo, another of his perversions of normal religious rituals (Aldrete, 2019). For the young man, it was just another day, doing whatever pleased him, enjoying everything his way. But tensions behind the scenes were rife with the prospect of his death.

There are a few different versions of his death, each one brutal:

- Oblivious to the plans in motion, he returned to the palace to gorge on lunch. When he entered, instead of servants attending to his desires, Chaerea was there with a contingent of his officers. They rushed him, stabbing Caligula to death 30 times.

- Another places Caligula talking to a band of boys who are about to perform. Chaerea snuck up behind him while he was distracted and slashed his neck, shouting out the traditional words accompanying a sacrifice: "Take this!" (Meddings, 2022). Cornelius Sabinus was there to finish things off by running his sword through the emperor.

- A third story has Sabinus distract Caligula by asking the password while the two men are in a passageway beneath the theater. Chaerea leaps out with a cry, swinging his sword and splitting open Caligula's jaw. While the emperor writhes on the floor, trying to get back up, others rush in to finish him off, stabbing him to death.

Whichever one can be believed, they all speak of the same brutality, feature the same conspirators, and arrive at the same end! The actions that follow are equally violent, displaying how vengeful they were and determined to rid Rome of its emperor. Claiming they were destroying his bloodline and there being any future chance of someone with his genes taking the throne again, the colluders hacked off Caligula's genitals. They went a step further and slew his wife before picking up his baby daughter and throwing her against a wall until she was dead.

After four years, Rome's leader lay in a pool of blood, his family cut down along with him. Instead of a lavish funeral procession, he was thrown into a shallow grave, and his uncle was thrust onto the throne. Claudius, Caligula's uncle, was not a willing replacement, having been found cowering in the palace at the time of the murder, but he was the only surviving relative fit for the job.

A Tarnished Legacy

Caligula lives on, not as a god or a glorified emperor of Rome, but as a depraved lunatic. It's a close call between him and Nero over who claims the top spot for the most infamous emperor, both living on in history books for the unbelievable tales of cruelty and perversion.

The question of the validity of the stories is still a debated point among historians today. Many believe that a concerted effort was made to smear Caligula's name by the senators who suffered under his rule. It justified their own actions in having to remove such an unfit ruler. Suetonius, the historian tasked with writing the accounts, goes to great lengths to paint a very dark and disturbing picture of the young man, even though other reports at the time do not exactly match up with his. However, his is one of the only sources history has to go by, and it does little to lift up the name of Caligula.

Deranged through illness or drunk on his power and wealth, he remains a fascinating figure who caused so much controversy in such a short time.

Chapter 4:

Domitian's Authoritarian Rule

Unfortunate is the fate of the principals, because they will not believe reports of the plot until they are murdered
–Domitian

The guests arrive at the palace, each one a notable dignitary. Not just any evening, this was billed as a lavish feast to honor those senators who held power and place in Rome. The elite of the elite made their way into a darkened room, everything black from the drapes to the tableware. A macabre atmosphere settled over the banquet room as they were met with an even more sinister detail. On the table, in front of every chair was a slab of stone, a tombstone inscribed with each guest's name.

The host welcomed them with a sly grin as he spoke of death. A foreboding sense of fear lingered in the air as each person wondered if this night would be their last. Swallowing each mouthful, trying to smile as the emperor continued his talk of the hereafter, there was a hurried exit as the meal was finally declared finished. But the ominous evening continued as the senators arrived home to find a gift waiting for them. A small slab, just like the one at the banquet, with their name clearly written as a reminder.

A sick joke? A threat? An elaborate sense of theater? A reminder of who was in control?

Domitian's reign as ruler of the Western nation had a few highlights, but it was the dark, somber tyranny that hung across Rome that would be this emperor's eulogy.

Inauspicious Beginnings

Born on 24 October, 51 CE on Pomegranate Street in the heart of Rome, his mother died while he was fairly young, leaving him in the care of his uncle, Sabinus, while his father and brother were off fighting (Wasson, 2013). Although he enjoyed the privilege of having both a father and a brother as emperors, Domitian's upbringing was hardly on track for him to become ruler of Rome. As the youngest brother, he was overlooked and not even considered for a role in politics!

Although he seemed a bright child, he was not given the court education that his older brother, Titus, enjoyed. He was not old enough to join the military and was left behind as civil war raged on. Fending for himself most of the time, he became so poor that the historian Suetonius described him as having a "rather degraded youth" (Wasson, 2013). Domitian kept to himself and was considered something of a loner and recluse. Not exactly emperor material!

But he would find himself next in line to rule once the Flavian Dynasty had been established. Vespasian, his father, had been busy for most of Domitian's upbringing, focused on establishing his name across the nation. Having had a good relationship with Emperor Claudius, Vespasian was appointed consul and secured good standing until the ruler died, and things went cold. For almost a decade under the next emperor, Nero, Vespasian was not involved in any politics, but he was finally given command of the soldiers tasked with stamping out the Jewish revolt. When Nero died, there was a rush for the throne, resulting in what was known as the Year of Four Emperors, which ended when Vitellius, a general, rose up and seized power (Moore & McCormick, 2003).

A civil war broke out as Vespasian declared himself emperor, turning his forces on his opponent. Vitellius responded by besieging Rome and setting fire to the temple that Domitian had been hiding in. The young boy only managed to survive by dressing up as a priestess and escaping across the Tiber. It was only when Flavian forces recaptured the city and killed Vitellius that Domitian returned in the company of armed forces.

For a brief period, while his father and brother were still returning, he was seen as the representative of the imperial family of Flavius. Although he made few real decisions, he was called "Caesar" until Vespasian arrived to assume his place as emperor. Even then, Domitian was given hardly any responsibilities, sidelined by Titus who was the favored heir to the throne.

Vespasian ruled from 69 – 76 CE, and he was a very shrewd manager compared to Nero. When he died, Titus immediately stepped in to take his rightful place (Wasson, 2013). But the older brother would not sit long in Rome's highest office; Domitian rushed back to claim the title of ruler before Titus had even breathed his last. Stories of how the emperor met his end range from a fever that was contracted on a journey, to Domitian poisoning him, and even a story in the Talmud of a gnat flying up his nose and chewing on his brain after he destroyed the Temple in Jerusalem (Hoekstra, 2021).

Titus's last words, "I have made but one mistake" (Wasson, 2013) may have meant nothing, but they also could have been a portent of things to come. Historians have alluded to it being because he may have had an affair with Domitian's wife, although she denied this. It may have been his regret at not having killed his brother when he had the chance, realizing what a threat Domitian had become.

Delivering the Goods

As with Caligula and Nero, Domitian's reign in 81 CE began well. He was good at administrating and saw to the people's needs. Taxes were adjusted, and public order rose to a new high as his meticulous approach to justice brought calm to the city and outlying regions. Generally, he was viewed as a capable and likable emperor.

Ironically, he set new laws in place to bring morality back to the people. Male castration was outlawed, and any senators who practiced homosexuality were publicly reprimanded. When it came to incest, he made an example of the Vestal Virgins for their crime, sentencing them to death. Suetonius remarked that during this time, the officials' "standard of restraint and justice was never higher" (Hoekstra, 2021).

Building projects saw much of Rome that had been damaged by fire became rebuilt under Domitian's watch. The Capitol was restored, and a new temple to Jupiter and a concert hall were constructed. The Colosseum, which had begun before his time, was finally finished with a special basement floor designed to be able to host mock naval battles. The existing palace was pulled down and a new one rose up in its place, called the Flavian Palace. The Stadium of Domitian was made as a gift to the Roman public and saw the first of the Capitoline Games in 86 CE (Hoekstra, 2021). All in all, the structural beauty of the city flourished under him as he saw more than 50 buildings finished.

The Colosseum

When it came to the military, Domitian was not like his father, Vespasian, or brother, Titus; he lacked the skills of tactical strategy. Despite this, he prided himself on being able to advise his generals by sending them messages when they were on the frontline. When the chance to lead a campaign came along in 83 CE, he jumped at it, and he successfully brought the Chatti to surrender; however, it was not due to any of his commands. Other wars between the Dacians and Sarmatians were fought, but they were not outright victories. His biggest military accomplishment was not on the battlefield but rather in raising the pay of soldiers, an act that won him the popularity of legionaries everywhere.

One of Domitian's interests lay in poetry, even though he had no formal training in the art. Appearing in public to recite poems, he also added contests to certain games to highlight and reward this particular indulgence of his. However, having seen how Nero's efforts at being deigned a singing superstar backfired and became a reason for his downfall, Domitian gave up any aspirations as a poet, giving the excuse that he was too busy with administrative duties.

True Colors

The emperor may have brought order, may have enacted on good advice, and may even have won the hearts and minds of the military, but there were troubling signs that soon became evidence of a more troubled personality clutching onto his power.

Sitting alone in his room for hours, he focused on one odd, sadistic hobby. Using a thin, sharpened stylus that would have been his pen, Domitian would kill flies. He would patiently sit, watching the insects as they buzzed around the room, waiting for one to land somewhere close before spearing it with his weapon. It happened so often, that when anyone asked if there was anyone in the room with him, the response was "Not even a fly!" (Suetonius et al., 2014).

This callous viciousness became an underlying theme of Domitian's reign. Even when dispensing justice, although he seemed good at it, the measures of discipline that came with it were sometimes rather excessive. In defiance of the Senate, he let the Vestal Virgins choose their own punishment, having them burned and clubbed to death, while Cornelia, the main Vestal Virgin was entombed alive (Moore & McCormick, 2003).

Having been denied position and status for so long, it is no surprise that he had a penchant for taking what belonged to others. Having had a string of lovers as a youngster, when it came to marriage, his eye was on Domitia, a married woman. The emperor's solution was simple:

force her to divorce and marry him. However, when she was accused of having an affair, he banished her and took up with Titus 'daughter, his own niece, only to run back into the arms of his wife. None of this prevented him from what he called "bed-wrestling," where he entertained concubines and prostitutes (Suetonius et al., 2014).

Although he preferred being on his own, hardly going out at night, he was not shy to enjoy a good party, banquet, or chariot game. In fact, his lavish spending on these caused an alarming deficit in the economy as he threw money at the gaudiest celebrations. Sweets and coins rained down on spectators during games and festivals, but his greatest entertainment expense came when he invited guests to dine with him. Themed feasts spread over a thousand tables, laden with figs, dates, nuts, and other sumptuous foods that were brought in from distant provinces, especially for the occasions. His ominous death meal has become synonymous with Domitian's harsh cruelty and disturbing sense of pleasure.

This, coupled with the increased pay to soldiers and extensive building programs, drained the budget very quickly. After the first few years of having plenty to splash out, he had to resort to other measures to continue subsidizing his lifestyle and plans. His answer was to raise the Jewish taxes and seize land and money from the rich, particularly senators for whom he did not hide his dislike.

There was no love lost between the Senate and the emperor. Unlike his father, who had to carefully nurture support from the most powerful men in Rome in order to establish his place as ruler, Domitian did not need any of that. His dynastic line was already intact when he assumed the throne, and he saw little need for the meddling of the Republic. Wasson (2013) shows the lengths he was willing to push his own powers as a despot:

> The Senate was almost stripped entirely of its power and his paranoia led to the execution of both senators and imperial officers for the most trivial of offenses. Out of jealousy, he had Sullustius Lucullus, governor of Britannia, executed for naming a new type of lance after himself.

This increasing paranoia became the core reason for his harsh dealings with offenders and anyone else he deemed a threat. While he hoped that wielding an iron fist in his ramped-up treason trials would frighten off people who may have thought of overthrowing him, the opposite was true. At least eleven senators who held the rank of consul were butchered, with many others being banished from the city (Moore & McCormick, 2003). The tension between Domitian and the Senate only fueled suspicions and schemes to put a stop to the brutality.

The emperor's distrust and fear of anyone and everyone led him to adopt extreme measures. As well as being heavily guarded wherever he went, the palace walls were laid with a special "shining" phengite stone that was polished to a high sheen so he could see his own reflection and anyone else who might be creeping up on him (Suetonius et al., 2014). He had his personal secretary killed because he had heard rumors that Nero's assistant had been involved in his murder. A firm believer in omens, Domitian consulted soothsayers and astrologers in an attempt to discern how to avoid any events that would end in death.

Informers were everywhere, spying out any possible rebellion or plot against the ruler, and anyone imprisoned had their hands cut off or genitals burned! While most of this may have been a trumped-up witch hunt brought on by unfounded distrust, there were those conspiring to overthrow Domitian, and in September of 87 CE, a group of senators were found guilty and executed (Wasson, 2013).

Vain Glory

Domitian's vanity was well known. Described by Suetonius (2014) as "handsome and graceful," the emperor had one flaw that caused him pain when pointed out in public. He was balding, very much like Caligula, and took it as a personal insult if it was mentioned. It became such an issue that he is thought to have written a book called *On the Care of the Hair*, which he dedicated to a friend (Hoekstra, 2021). But this may not be entirely true, as most of the writing of speeches and reports was delegated to others.

Agricola, an astute general who enjoyed numerous victories, was a particular irritation to Domitian. On the one hand, the man's wins on the battlefield were good for Rome as a whole, but, on a personal level, they showed the emperor's own lack as a military strategist. As a plan to remove him from the public eye, Domitian recalled him from the frontlines and offered the general the position of governor in faraway Syria. In the end, Agricola died an untimely death, which caused suspicions to surface over his untimely passing.

This conceit was taken to a new level when Domitian expected and enjoyed being called "*dominus et deus*" (master or god) by his subjects (Wasson, 2013). While this act caused such a stir of anger when Caligula had tried to set himself up as a deity, by the time of Domitian's rule, the deification of a living emperor was not that strange, although not openly accepted by the Senate. He did not stop there, renaming two calendar months after himself and setting up so many gold and silver statues that on one of the sculptures, someone scratched the graffiti slogan, "It is enough!" (Suetonius et al., 2014).

Pliny the Younger (Franz, 1999) wrote about this god-like belief:

> He [Domitian] was a madman, blind to the true meaning of his position, who used the arena for collecting charges of high treason, who felt himself slighted and scorned if we failed to pay homage to his gladiators, taking any criticism of them to himself and seeing insults to his own godhead and divinity; who deemed himself the equal of the gods yet raised his gladiators to his equal. (para. 10)

This god-like cult Domitian had set up for himself, to the point of building temples and having citizens in outlying provinces forced to honor and worship his statues, drew criticism. One such voice was the Apostle John. To quieten the voice of this Christian leader, the emperor had him exiled in 95 CE to the island of Patmos, where John would write one of the most famous books of the Bible: Revelation (Franz, 1999). In elaborate style, the book displays vivid, allegorical images of a ruler who sets himself up as a god in defiance of the one and only true God. While terrifying, it is also a story of hope for those who were enduring persecution at the hands of Romans because it carries a prediction of the downfall of such emperors.

A Predictable End

Suetonius described Domitian as "cruel," "cunning," "greedy for money," and his reign as an "object of terror to all" (Moore & McCormick, 2003). The final act of taking down such a vicious control freak is telling because there were suggestions that even his wife, Domitia, knew about it and approved since she was in fear for her own life. Nobody felt safe around the emperor, not even himself!

Having heard that their names were on a list of some sort that Domitian had, a group huddled in a knot of conspiracy as they tried to decide on whether the bath or the dining room table should be the scene of their crime. A member of Domitian's staff, Stephanus, who was also living on borrowed time because of accusations against him, approached these men who had gathered in the shadows with another idea.

Getting close to the emperor would always be tricky, but Stephanus ' plan involved "injuring" his arm and having it wrapped up. This was where the dagger was hidden, between the folds of cloth. After several days of this act, with no one suspecting him of anything untoward, he came forward with details and names of a plot against Domitian.

Meanwhile, Domitian, a superstitious man, had gobbled up the prediction he received that he would be killed on the sixth hour of September 18 (Meddings, 2022). What he failed to understand was that it was only part of the plot. After doubling the guard and taking all precautions, the hour came and went, and Domitian, sensing he was in the clear, dismissed his attendants. Alone in his room, he saw no danger in allowing one of his staff in to bring him a message.

When Stephanus was ushered in, he came close enough to whisper and pulled out the concealed weapon. Stabbing the ruler in his groin, Domitian was visibly stunned. A struggle followed as the emperor tried to grab his own knife that he always kept close, but on that day, it was not there. Soon, the other members of the group rushed in and finished the job, hacking at their target until he was dead.

The Flavian Dynasty came to an end with Domitian's death on 18 September, 96 C.E (Wasson, 2013). Wasting little time in their joy at having their archenemy removed from power, the Senate grabbed ladders and began pulling down votive shields, statues, and anything else that bore the emperor's name, smashing them to the ground. This was part of them enacting the decree of "*damnatio memoriae*" which meant they could eliminate any existence of Domitian from public record (Hoekstra, 2021).

The city celebrated by trashing ceremonial arches and sculptures dedicated to the dead ruler. The Roman Army, however, mourned the loss of an emperor who they saw as having taken care of them and looked out for their interests. It is no surprise then, that even though many were jubilant over the end of the 15-year reign of terror, the conspirators who had a hand in bringing Domitian down were rooted out by the Praetorian Guard and killed.

In a quick fix to fill the vacancy since Domitian had no heir, an older man named Nerva was given the job. He would be the first of what would come to be known as the "Five Good Emperors" who ruled from 98 – 196 CE.

Chapter 5:

Commodus: The Militant Gladiator

I alone was born for you in the imperial palace.
—Commodus

Cassius Dio, the historian, sees Commodus 'rule as the beginning of the end when he says, "For our history now descends from a kingdom of gold to one of iron and rust" (Johns, 2020b).

One of the most well-known Roman emperors because of the Ridley Scott movie, *Gladiator,* Commodus comes off as a cunning, spiteful, self-indulgent ruler who enjoyed nothing more than the sight of blood. Although the film is not entirely accurate, it paints him as a disappointment to his father, showing Commodus to be someone who loved the attention of the crowds, and a man with a vengeful streak is not far from the truth.

That the entire movie revolves around gladiators is also not merely an artistic stretch, since Commodus enjoyed nothing more than to be in the arena himself, beating others with his sword to the cheer of thousands. But there are a few holes that can be filled in to get a fuller picture of someone who was probably not fit to take the throne at all. Taking over from a true statesman and philosophical man like his father, Marcus Aurelius, was always going to be a tough act to follow.

The problem was that Commodus could never have met the expectations that had been set for him, even if he had tried. Looking at the reports and accounts of the time, it becomes clearer that Commodus was born into royalty but had little to no skill in politics. He had a head for fun, pleasure, and cruelty. To that end, many see his reign as the end of the golden age of the Roman Empire.

A Disappointment

Unlike any other emperor, Commodus bore the distinct honor of being the only one who was "born in the purple," a term describing an heir who was purely biological (Healy, n.d.). Every other ruler, including his father, had taken the throne by force, was nominated by the Senate, or had been adopted into the royal family to aid their succession. Even Domitian did not enjoy this right, since his father was not yet emperor at the time of his birth.

Born just outside of Rome on 31 December, 161 CE, he was the tenth of twelve children and ended up being the next in line since he was the only son eligible after his twin brother, Titus died when he was four years old (Cavazzi, 2021). Although he was given the best in education, Commodus showed very little aspirations when it came to those subjects that were fit for an emperor. Instead of matters of court, diplomacy, and philosophy, he was more inclined to dance, sing, and mold goblets from clay. His favorite, though, was to play at being a gladiator, something he would continue into adulthood.

Perhaps he was spoiled and doted upon by his father, who chose to be blind to all Commodus' shortcomings, but there were signs from an early age that his tendencies were not lining up with those of a balanced politician. One story is of a 12-year-old Commodus who throws a vicious tantrum when he finds his bath water is not hot enough. The young boy orders the servant who filled the bath to be thrown into a furnace, and his anger is only sated when a sheepskin is burned, instead, to give the idea and satisfaction that his commands have been obeyed (Fagan, 2017).

Turning a Blind Eye

Marcus Aurelius, the stoic leader, gave his son every opportunity to grow into his future role. But even in this, Commodus seems to have been able to twist his father's arm or deceive him into doing what he wanted. The *Historia Augusta* (Thayer, n.d.) describes his approach to tutors in the following way:

The more honorable of those appointed to supervise his life he could not endure, but the most evil he retained, and, if any were dismissed, he yearned for them even to the point of falling sick. When they were reinstated through his father's indulgence, he always maintained eating houses and low resorts for them in the imperial palace. He never showed regard for either decency or expense. (para. 4)

As if that was not enough, his carousing and hedonistic lifestyle was already in full swing by this stage: gambling with dice in his house, keeping numerous prostitutes in his room, wandering around the markets, hanging out with charioteers and gladiators, and behaving more like a servant than a prince (Thayer, n.d.). To all this, his father never said a word or saw fit to bring him back into line.

As part of his grooming to be emperor, Marcus Aurelius took him along on military campaigns where he could gain some insight and knowledge. He was also made a junior emperor (Caesar) when he was only five, and later a joint emperor when he turned sixteen. The second nomination might have been more of an attempt to secure the throne after Cassius tried to usurp his position when he was falsely informed by Commodus 'mother that Marcus Aurelius had died. Even then, plans and plots were to subvert what others (his mother included) could see as a doomed reign if the boy became ruler.

Bust of Marcus Aurelius

While accompanying his father to oversee battles on the northern frontier, Marcus Aurelius died in 180 CE, possibly poisoned by Commodus (Catalano, 2000). Immediately the 19-year-old returned to Rome and assumed his rightful place over the empire. Showing none of the work ethic and interest in government that was supposedly in his genes, some historians have even wondered if he was a legitimate heir after all, bolstering their argument on whispers of Commodus' mother being involved in many extra-marital affairs (Cavazzi, 2021a). Either way, a young tyrant who had no inkling or desire for administrating or affairs of state took the throne.

Different Priorities

It did not take long for Commodus, the 18th emperor of Rome, to make changes. The new emperor returned to the capital in glory with all the regal pomp he could, as though he had won the victories. His first act was to cease all military actions near the Danube, a major campaign that Marcus Aurelius had thrown all his effort into. Whether it was a strategic move, or the fact that Commodus wanted to get back to Rome as fast as possible and enjoy the delights the city held for him, a truce was signed, and the frontier lines that had been fought so hard for were discarded.

Although he made promises to continue what his father had started, this was quickly rescinded, and the forces were withdrawn. The reality was that he oversaw no military campaigns during his time on the throne, the borders of the empire in relative peace. When it came to all other matters of state, Commodus was not interested. According to Dio (Fagan, 2017), it was not because he did not care, but because he was "unintelligent, lacked guile, and was easily manipulated." A weak-willed man left the door open for others to rule in his place.

Deferred Power

Commodus's lack of political acumen and complete detachment from affairs of state defines his reign as one where power was up for grabs to whoever was the favorite at the time, or whoever could manipulate the emperor and situations. Commodus was surrounded by people hungry for power and recognition, and a series of men climbed over each other to hold onto this spot so they could set themselves up and benefit from their decisions.

The job of administration first fell to Aelius Saoterus, a Greek adviser and very close friend. So close, that as Commodus rode on his chariot in his triumphal procession, he kissed Saoterus a number of times during the festivities. This arrangement of having someone else handle the affairs of the state while their leader caroused and cavorted caused the Senate a huge headache. After a couple of years, Saoterus found himself on the out, quietly removed and dealt with by the Praetorian Guard.

At this time, Commodus 'inaction had also caused him to lose favor, and a conspiracy to overthrow his reign was hatched by none other than his own sister, Annia Lucilla, in 182 CE (Cavazzi, 2021a). It was a simple plot that would have been successful, except that the man they chose to strike the fatal blow was more interested in making a statement than getting the job done. Lying in wait, as Commodus entered the Colosseum, he jumped out brandishing a blade. Instead of striking quickly, he shouted that he'd been sent by the Senate to kill the emperor, which gave the guards enough time to rush and tackle him to the ground (Fagan, 2017).

This caused him to wake up enough to see that he needed someone stronger to run things for him while he wasted away his days and nights in pleasure. A Praetorian Prefect, Perennis was assigned the task of running the country in Commodus' absence, doing so for seven years. He wielded his power much like Sejanus had under Tiberius, weeding out any opposition and cunningly stacking things in his own favor, until he was seen as getting too close to taking the throne itself. His own Praetorian Guard ended up executing him and his family.

A man named Cleander, once a slave, was next to take the reins, conveniently having had a hand in Perennis 'downfall. This new administrator's greed reached new heights as he sold public offices to the highest bidders and eliminated any and every opposition with brutal efficiency. But just as he had orchestrated Perennis 'downfall, he, too, was set up when the grain commissioner cut off all supply of grain in

190 CE, blaming it on Cleander (Cavazzi, 2021a). A riot ensued, and Commodus gave the people the head of his right-hand man to appease the mob.

Finally, and a little reluctantly, Commodus took over the running of the country himself. However, as Fagan (2017) points out, this period between 1892 and 192 CE was one of the most disastrous in the history of Rome and "demonstrates that Commodus was deeply unsuited for power."

Good but Not Great

One of Commodus 'greatest pleasures was gladiator fighting. He not only grabbed every chance he could to watch the performances but regularly appeared in the Colosseum to take part in the spectacles. As a left-handed swordsman, he was not bad, able to wield a weapon easily enough. Parts of the imperial palace were renovated to include an area where he could practice. While he used a sharp blade during these private bouts, often hurting, maiming, and even killing opponents, only blunt instruments were used when he fought in front of the crowds.

Unlike the movie, which sees him take one last fight against a fictional antagonist named Maximus, Commodus was no stranger to the bloodied sands of the arena, clocking up an impressive 735 appearances. He seldom missed an opportunity to show off his skills. Senators and officials were forced to come and watch every time he made his way out and had to chant victorious cries. If that was not debasing enough for them, the Roman Treasury had to pay him 25,000 silver pieces for each one of his gaudy shows—his fee for performing (Catalano, 2000).

Gladiator equipment

Unlike the regal entrance portrayed in the movie, Commodus often stripped himself down to a loin cloth and strode barefoot into the arena, a very un-emperor-like thing to do. But he was no stranger to hanging out with chariot racers and gladiators as if he were one of them, enjoying their company to those of the senators. Once he killed an opponent, Commodus would happily smear the slain man's blood on his clothes and his hair, parading himself as a worthy champion as he went back home. While he was an adequate swordsman, his victories were not all due to skill. The historian, Herodian (Catalano, 2000), tells it like it is when he says:

> In his gladiatorial combats, he defeated his opponents with ease, and he did no more than wound them, since they all submitted to him, but only because they knew he was the emperor, not because he was truly a gladiator. (para. 12)

When it came to the bow and arrow and javelin, Commodus showed incredible marksmanship. Importing beasts to Rome to be set free as targets or as predators was a favorite for the spectators. The emperor took part in these instances, although he was safely at a distance out of harm's way when he did. Whether it was lions, leopards, giraffes, or bears, he shot them all, even tallying up a stunning 100 kills in one day (Catalano, 2000). When a flock of ostriches was released, he used crescent-headed arrows to take off their heads, the crowd cheering as they ran headless in the Colosseum. But the senators were appalled as their leader strutted around, waving one of the bloodied bird heads in the air.

When one gladiator showed how good he was at piercing a lion with his javelin while riding horseback, Commodus had him executed out of sheer jealousy. In another bizarre moment, he ordered some of Rome's cripples to be dressed up like snake monsters and gave them sponges as weapons. He took great pleasure in shooting at them and having them clubbed to death.

Since gladiators were deemed nothing more than prostitutes or servants, to see the emperor of Rome joining in these festivities was very difficult for many who held office in the city. It was debasing to watch him throw away his name and reputation so easily, and it caused many to wish that this madman's antics would come to an end.

Thinking Too Highly of Himself

While many saw his actions as ridiculous and below the standards fit for a ruler of his stature, Commodus began to see himself in a new light. Once he took back power, he did so draped in a lion's skin and brandishing a club, declaring that he was Hercules. This concept of being god was not new; Nero, Caligula, and Domitian had all done exactly the same, setting themselves up as gods. But while the Senate put up with it in public, they did not support it in private, and it caused many to conspire to find ways to remove this self-proclaimed deity.

What followed was a vain attempt at glorifying himself throughout the city by erecting statues in his likeness, one of solid gold that weighed close to 1,000 pounds (Dimuro, 2022). Not content with this, Commodus proceeded to change the calendar months to reflect his great characteristics. After a fire burnt through much of the city, he was able to rebuild it to his own liking, and the name of the city was no longer to be Rome but became *Colonia Commodiana* (Colony of

Commodus). Jerusalem suffered a similar fate of being renamed, and he proceeded to rename all the prominent buildings after himself so that it was clear it all belonged to him.

Declaring he was Romulus, an official edict was sent out that his rule was to be known as "The Golden Age" (Catalano, 2000). Whatever gold was left in the treasury was dished out to the public and the army in a bid to keep them distracted and happy. The wealthy, though, were taxed to keep up with his spending habits.

And, just like his predecessors, he forced the Senate to recognize him as a deity, believing he was truly the reincarnation of Hercules. And, as a jeer to those emperors, he replaced the head of one of Nero's statues with his own, inscribing beneath it: "The only left-handed fighter to conquer twelve times (as I recall the number) one thousand men" (Dimuro, 2022).

While he had been disinterested in matters of state, happy to delve into depravity rather than bore himself with politics and administration, things had at least continued to run. The governing of Rome may have been riddled with corruption, bribery, and scheming, but without Commodus interfering, the Senate managed to have some sort of voice. The embarrassment of having an emperor run around almost naked and barefoot in the Colosseum was enough to bear without him also bungling the day-to-day affairs.

With him taking control, dressed as a lion, the circus moved from the arena into the Curia, the meeting place of the Senate. Instead of allowing Commodus to think he was the best gladiator, he went further and began to laude his belief of being divine over everyone. Romans had no trouble deifying dead emperors, but a living one was a step too far.

His megalomania had reached such a point that people (especially those in the Senate, who had to pander to his every whim and fear for their own lives) wanted him gone. Twelve years of having him as emperor had become too much to bear, and a plot was hatched to bring about a change.

Ending the Gladiator's Reign

Commodus had just finished up another one of his many performances in the arena, fighting as a gladiator and killing off a number of wild beasts while elevated up on a platform. With the city in chaos and verging on bankruptcy, the senators knew that things could not continue if they wanted to save any of their nation's respectability. "Commodus was a greater curse to the Romans than any pestilence or any crime" (Dimuro, 2022). He had to go.

Things came to a head when Commodus, swimming in his delusions of grandeur and divinity, announced that on 1 January 193 CE, he would usher in the year as consul and gladiator (Fagan, 2017). The Senate could not bear the embarrassment any longer, and plans were set in motion. Those closest to the emperor began plotting, mainly because they believed their lives were at stake since they had heard their names had been added to Commodus' list of people he wanted executed.

Among this group was Aemilius Laetus, the Praetorian prefect who was advising the ruler, Commodus' own chamberlain, Eclectus, and Marcia, the mistress. The scheme seemed simple enough, but, as with others that had gone before, it almost backfired, and they had to resort to a rudimentary backup plan in the end.

Whether Marcia slipped poison into his wine, or the beef he ate was laced with it, Commodus ingested enough of it to kill a man. Instead, he vomited it back up again and survived. Deciding he had probably had too much to drink, the emperor ordered a bath to be run. Seeing their plan had not worked, the conspirators turned to Narcissus, a wrestler who often sparred with Commodus. Some reports say it happened in the bath while others put the scene in the bedroom, but, in the end, they resorted to muscle to accomplish the deed. Narcissus strangled his wrestling partner to death and Rome could breathe a sigh of relief, knowing another madman was gone.

For a gladiator or a god, it was a rather abject way to go.

Tarnished Legacy

While Marcus Aurelius left behind a revered legacy as one of the best rulers in Roman history, the only tarnish to his name was to bequeath the top spot to his inept son. Commodus' poor attempts at taking up the reigns from where his father left off are a humiliating blemish on the calendar of such a long line of prestigious emperors. But his disgrace did not end when his life was suffocated from him.

The Senate did everything in its power to wipe out the name of the gladiator emperor from the empire, defacing statues, scratching out inscriptions, and even rewriting certain parts of history to vilify the 12 years of Commodus. The decree they issued to this effect was particularly damning:" Cast the gladiator into the charnel-house. He who slew the Senate, let him be dragged with the hook... Let the murderer be dragged in the dust!" (Johns, 2020b).

But even that would not be enough to right all the wrongs. Someone would need to fill the vacancy of running Rome, and that task was given to Pertinax, who did a relatively good job until he lost the support of the Praetorians and was murdered after only 86 days (Johns, 2020b). Civil war broke out as attempts were made to bring order back to the chaos Commodus had left behind. It would only come four years later when Septimus Severus, the first emperor of African descent, took the throne.

In a bizarre twist, instead of removing Commodus from memory, he was brought back to life when Severus claimed he was a descendant of the late Marcus Aurelius and therefore, related as a brother to Commodus. The failed emperor's body was exhumed, and he was deified.

Chapter 6:

Elagabalus: A Reign of Debauchery

I am emperor. It is I who know what is best for Rome.
Not you traitors.
–Elagabalus

A tiara encrusted with jewels sits atop the boy's fair head. His face is soft in the sunlight, with beautiful features that are almost feminine. Draped over his shoulders hangs a glossy robe of the deepest Syrian purple made from rare Chinese silk, with more gems sewn into the hem. As he walks slowly backward through the city, crowds that line the street stare, some not sure what this new festivity is all about, others transfixed by the figure leading the way. In the boy's hand are the reins of the six pure white horses. Attached to these fine animals is a chariot covered in ornate gold and silver with precious jewels embedded into the artwork.

It glimmers in the sunlight, but the object it carries also has a dark gleam to it. Inside, is the *baetyl*, a large black stone of incredible importance to the whole procession. A black conical rock, it is from a foreign city and is believed to be sacred. The boy walks in reverse, keeping his eyes fixed on the emblem, the face of his god.

Regal in his outfit, the youngster leads the horses carrying the sacred stone down toward the newly renovated temple. The entourage is made up of bodyguards, the cavalry, and dancing women accompanied by music played on flutes and drums. Images of other gods are included in the parade, but they are not given equal status, and this is also not normal.

While this may sound like many of the religious rituals held during the Roman era, this one had the stark contrast of belonging to a foreign doctrine, not recognized by those in the city. More than that, the boy leading the procession, donning the garb of high priest, was none other than the emperor himself.

Although the youngest ever to rule, Elagabalus was known more for his eccentricities when it came to his religion, his choice of clothes, and his orgies. Instead of being remembered for anything of imperial quality, he has gone down in history as a teenager with raging hormones who threw extravagant parties and ceremonies.

A Lie to Start

Julia Domna had the distinct veneration of being the wife of one emperor and the mother of another. Married to Septimus Severus, she regularly accompanied him to the frontlines and enjoyed a position of power. When her son, Caracalla, became ruler, she remained loyal and also joined him on military campaigns. However, she committed suicide on hearing that her son had been assassinated.

Statue of Caracalla

It was Domna's sister, Julia Maesa, who would prove to be the one shifting the political (and genealogical) lines in order for her grandson to one day take over as ruler. She had enjoyed a life of luxury as part of the royal family through her sibling, and, once Caracalla was no longer in the picture, she found herself ousted and back in her hometown of Emesa in Syria. Not one to be denied her "rightful" place in the palace, she began cultivating an opportunity to be able to return to the life she had enjoyed.

With two grandsons from each of her daughters and her close connection with the previous royal family, Maesa began to spread rumors of a dynastic lineage. Claiming an affair had taken place between the late emperor and her one daughter would mean his blood carried on to her child, Varius Avitus Bassianus, born in 204 CE (Gill, 2019). Although illegitimate, the fact that the son belonged to Caracalla would automatically place him with a chance of ruling according to the laws of the day.

To ensure the lie took root, Maesa bribed a few soldiers stationed in the town, who then also took up the rallying cry of the youngster being the rightful heir to the imperial throne. Further evidence of this family tree fib was how similar her grandson looked to Caracalla—he bore a striking resemblance to the previous emperor.

Backed by the Military

When Caracalla met his untimely end at the hands of assassins, the throne was open for the next eligible candidate. One of these was Macrinus, a newly appointed Praetorian prefect without any senatorial rank. His commanding position gave him enough power to compel the soldiers to declare him emperor in April 217 (Gill, 2019).

However, his skills as a leader were tested as he faced a number of defeats in campaigns in the east, leading to humiliating truces with the enemies. His unpopularity with the army increased when he introduced a two-tiered pay system for those serving under him. The rumors that had been steadily growing of another contender for the position of ruler caused a split, and scores of soldiers swore allegiance to the legal heir, Maesa's grandson, Bassianus.

Two opposing forces clashed in the Battle of Antioch to decide the rightful ruler. Bassianus, only a young teenager at the time, led his contingent from the front, an inspiring and almost divine picture of a future leader. Victory came easily to the boy on June 8 and Macrinus was killed when he was later caught fleeing (Gill, 2019). To ensure no further claim to the throne, Macrinus' son, who had been named co-emperor by his father, was also chased down, found, and killed. The way was wide open for Bassianus, the 14-year-old.

Angering the Senate

He may have garnered the praise and support of the legionaries, but Bassianus began on the wrong foot with the ruling powers that made up the Senate. One of their functions was to sanction the new emperor in person, in Rome. However, Bassianus did not see the need, and, without waiting for approval from the Senate, the young boy assumed the name Marcus Aurelius Antoninus Augustus, a combination of all the best rulers, and the same as his predecessor, Caracalla.

He had declared himself emperor, a move that did not sit well with those back in the capital. The young boy would further infuriate and shock those of high standing by forcing the idea of him as a priest down their throats. Instead of rushing back, he and his family stayed the winter at Nicomedia. During that time, he sent a portrait of himself in his priestly outfit that was to be placed above the statue of Victory in the Curia, the Senate's meeting hall (Johns, 2020a).

Things soured even more when he finally arrived back and allowed his mother and grandmother into the Senate meetings with him. Traditional Roman conservatism held a very high regard for keeping the status quo, and the young boy's indifference to the way things worked irked the upper class. The 26th emperor had gotten his reign off to a rocky start.

Faith, Fetish, and Fun

For a youngster, one would have thought that he had sound counsel to advise and guide him in the ways and manners of the capital. His mother was always there right by his side, often taking part in Senate meetings, much to the chagrin of the officials, and his grandmother, Julia Maesa, was never far, but the new emperor proved to be more stubborn or more intent on doing what he wanted to abide by wise words.

Rather than keeping his oddities and desires under wraps, Bassianus, who came to be known as Elagabalus, was flagrant in his actions. It seems that, rather than being concerned with what others thought, he deliberately did things to poke at the order of the day.

Divine Contentions

Worshiping the sun was not a new religion, but one that dated back to Egyptian times and even before then when early man revered the golden orb that brought light and warmth to the earth. In a pantheon of deities, there would have been a place for such adoration since there were many to choose from and pray to. But there was a definite hierarchy regarding these divinities, each falling in very neatly beneath superior beings such as Jupiter in Rome and Zeus in Greece. Altering that ladder of belief was tantamount to blasphemy.

Having grown up on the outskirts of the Roman Empire, Bassianus was firmly entrenched in the belief that was practiced in Emesa, Syria. Bassianus had even been accepted as a priest in its order. The faith revolved around Elagabal, the Phoenician sun god who, unlike most other gods, had no human form. Since no statue could represent Elagabal's form, a large, black, pointed stone became the idol to worship (John, 2020a).

Born Bassianus, renamed when he assumed the place of emperor, this young boy has become known by the nickname according to his zealous dedication to his duties as a priest. Elagabalus was a 14-year-old who looked to topple Jupiter from his pedestal and replace him with something else.

During his time in Emesa, the soldiers there were entertained as they watched the eccentric dancing and rituals of this religion. They thought nothing of the little "Elagabalus" all dressed up in his robes. But when he brought everything along with him to Rome and suddenly had untold authority to do and say what he wanted, it was no longer a sideshow.

A new temple was constructed on Palatine Hill to house the sacred rock, and Elagabalus appointed himself as high priest of the order. This dual office of emperor and cleric was not a welcome one, especially since the boy spent more time attending ceremonies and rites than being concerned with matters of state. He was often seen parading around in his purple robes, sparkling tiara, and other jewelry, and he enjoyed making the senators watch as he danced and performed to a noise of drums and flutes. As Dio (Wasson, 2013) describes:

> The offense consisted, not in his introducing a foreign god into Rome or in his exalting in very strange ways, but in his placing him even before Jupiter himself and causing himself to be voted his priest.... Furthermore, he was frequently seen even in public clad in the barbaric dress that the Syrian priests use, and this had as much to do as anything with his receiving the nickname of "The Assyrian." (para. 7)

As part of his priestly rite, he underwent circumcision, a practice that was frowned upon by Greeks and Romans, who distinguished themselves from other civilizations that did (Mijatovic, 2012). The ire of the people was brought to a boiling point when he decided to move the fire of Vesta, the Palladium, and the shields of Salii to the new temple, as well as forcing Jews and Christians to only practice their rituals there (Magie, 1921). His hope of bringing all beliefs under one roof was met with fierce resistance.

Elagabalus was not unaware of the waves he was causing by throwing his new god into the sea of other deities. His grandmother had cautioned him before his return to Rome, sharing her concerns over what the Roman senators and public would make of the emperor's unconventional devotion. Instead of heeding advice, and rather than playing it safe, he made as big a splash as he could by shoving it in their faces. It would be one of many things that began to stack up against him.

Different Tendencies

Running rampant through the city, using it as an outlet for sexual release and experimentation seems to have come with the territory for many emperors who found themselves with power and raging hormones. Throwing a 14-year-old boy into this den of iniquity may have been asking for trouble, but that is not why he is remembered. His fetishes stretched beyond those of Caligula and Nero, pushing the boundaries of what was acceptable, or at least what the public was willing to turn a blind eye to.

In a bid to keep everyone happy and try to soften the blow of the religious upheaval that had been unleashed on Rome, Elagabalus was advised to marry into an aristocratic family. This would not only be better for his reputation but also for his tenuous claim to the throne. Julia Paula became the first of many wives to pass through the palace, although she would not stay long, as the emperor dissolved the nuptials when he found a blemish of some kind on her body (Wasson, 2013a).

During his four years in power, Elagabalus was married six times, one of those to a Vestal Virgin, which caused an uproar. He divorced her after public pressure but ended up taking her back again, defending his actions of sleeping with her by saying "I did it in order that godlike children might spring from me" (Wasson 2013a).

But his effeminate mannerisms leaned toward having lots of men around him, hiring members of his court based on the size of their genitals and not their other talents. One such man was an athlete, Zoticus, who was discovered and quickly hurried off to Rome to the delight of Elagabalus. But the night did not go as planned because Hierocles, a charioteer and long-time partner of the emperor, drugged the well-endowed Zoticus so he could not perform and found himself thrown out the next morning (Grout, n.d.).

Although homosexuality was not openly condoned from those of high standing, the fact that it carried on was common knowledge. Elagabalus took it to extremes, though, when he swapped roles and began dressing up as a woman. Not just donning clothes like some had done before, but plucking his body, applying make-up, and wearing a wig, he would roam through the streets at night in his female disguise, looking for sexual partners of any sex and any proclivity.

Dio, the historian, goes so far as to suggest that the young emperor was so desperate to please his male counterparts that he offered physicians huge sums of money if they could use incisions to somehow create a vagina for him (Mijatovic, 2012). Elagabalus deeply desired to castrate himself, but there is no record of him having this operation, and many historians claim that much of this never happened and was only a way of discrediting the emperor.

When it came to orgies, they were nothing new to the palace, but Elagabalus introduced innovative ways to make them more exciting and sensual. He took them to a whole new level by adding heaps of rose petals for people to leap naked into and carouse around as if they were a bed of flowers. Servants were on standby to keep adding more petals to the writhing mass of bodies, some unable to crawl out of the mound, apparently smothered to death by roses!

Whichever way he swung, Elagabalus was certainly known for his penchant for sex, and, even if the stories are pared back, they still paint him as a youngster who ran wild through the halls of the palace and the streets of Rome.

Strange Tastes

Newfound authority can sometimes go to a person's head, especially in a teenager who is still developing a sense of diplomacy, right and wrong, restraint, and other adult qualities. These do not seem to be characteristics portrayed by Elagabalus. His morbid sense of fun would see him abuse his power simply to amuse himself. His silly antics ranged from ordering staff to collect 1,000 pounds of spider webs or 1,000 weasels, or having a chariot pulled by lions or naked women

(Bernett, 2020). He even had snakes released into the Colosseum where the spectators were seated just to see the reaction.

Like many of his predecessors, the emperor was expected to throw banquets for the wealthy and hold games for the greater public. Elagabalus never missed a chance to be eccentric and lavish in these instances. One dinner saw 600 ostrich heads being served to guests, while other times there was peacock tongue, camel heel, and flamingo brain on the menu (Bernett, 2020). Sometimes he went to the extreme by having real food served to himself and a mixture of inedible things served to guests.

A hands-on party planner, Elagabalus changed it up every dinner time, making the décor green one day, blue the next, and a sparkling array of colors on the following night. He would also get his guests involved by asking them to "invent new sauces for giving flavor to the food, and he would offer a very large prize for the man whose invention should please him, even presenting him with a silk garment" (Corletti, 2017).

Always playing the odds, the young boy began a kind of lottery that seemed to have been one of the only lasting things that carried on after his death. At his banquets, guests would find inscriptions engraved into their spoons with the prizes they had won. Some utensils would say "ten camels" or "ten pounds of gold" while unlucky people would find themselves with a gift of ten eggs or ten dead flies (Bernett, 2020). This idea was a favorite at the gladiator games where gifts of lettuce, coins, and even bears could be handed out.

When it came to spectacles, Elagabalus went the extra mile. Instead of flooding the Colosseum with water for a naval battle as had been done previously, he flooded a large area in the center of Rome with Falernian red wine! Another exhibition saw him race a chariot up a hill drawn by elephants, destroying ancient tombs in the process.

Gone Too Far

Elagabalus ended where he started, with his grandmother's conniving ways. Julia Maesa had done all the hard work to get her grandson onto the throne and, despite her advice and pulling strings to bring stability to his reign, he repeatedly went off script. His popularity plummeted with each action, each rumor, and every scandalous outfit he wore. He had incensed the Senate from the beginning and did little to appease them. The soldiers, who had once supported him, no longer wanted an effeminate boy running the show.

In a last-ditch attempt to right some of the wrongs, Maesa turned to her other grandson, 12-year-old Severus Alexander. Although rather docile, she realized that, without him in the running, she would lose her place in the palace. The plan to have Elagabalus adopt his own cousin as heir did not go down well, though, and ended up in a family rift with mother and aunt at loggerheads.

By this stage, the young emperor may have seen things were crumbling fast around him. If the history of Roman rulers was anything to go by, he needed to prepare for the worst. There were unsupported rumors that he had a scarlet and purple silk noose to hang himself if it came to that, a stash of golden swords should he have chosen that option, poisons laced with jewels for a fancy last drink, or even a tower with jewels in it to fling himself off. These may have been more a ridicule at the boy's behavior than his actual actions.

What Elagabalus did do, however, was order the Praetorian Guard to kill his cousin, Alexander, but by then he had lost every trace of respectability and authority. They refused even after he offered a bribe. Instead, they turned on him, slaughtering him on 11 March 222 CE as he hid in the toilets of the Praetorian camp with his mother.

To demonstrate how unpopular he was, they were both beheaded, mother and son. The corpses were then attached to hooks and dragged through the streets for all to see. The soldiers threw him into the sewer, but the bodies got stuck, so they hauled them out, tied stones to them, and dropped Elagabalus and his mother into the Tiber River. The shouts from the crowd echoed as one: "Elagabalus alone was worse than Commodus!" (Aldrete, 2020).

Calm After the Storm

With the self-indulged teenager out of the way, Rome sighed a collective breath, happy to see the back of one of the worst emperors. Four years of his reign proved to be too long for anyone else to endure except Elagabalus and his mother. Little came from his rule in the way of military campaigns, economic reform, or any other political decisions. His reign turned out to be one long sex-fest with a strange religion thrown into the mix.

Alexander Severus, the cousin of Elagabalus, became emperor. With his grandmother, the king-maker Maesa, and his mother to guide him, order was restored. He was still young, and, having seen what damage a young boy could do if he was let loose, the two women kept a firm hand on the new ruler. Jupiter found his place at the top of the list of gods again, and the Senate was welcomed back to engage in politics.

A period of relative stability returned to Rome under Alexander, who ruled for thirteen years even after Maesa died only two years into his reign.

Elagabalus 'anecdotes may seem like they come straight out of a drug-infused pornography movie. Although many historians discount many of the more sordid and over-the-top tales, ascribing those to the Senate and others doing their best to discredit an emperor they detested, there is truth to some of them. The young emperor certainly turned the Roman world upside down with some bizarre ideas and outlandish behavior, and, for those, he is remembered in infamy.

Chapter 7:

Honorius' Costly Indecision

It is better, of course, to know useless things than to know nothing.
–Seneca

Not all the Roman heads of state were debauched, mad, or evil. Some, like Honorius, never had what it took to be a ruler. Like certain emperors who came years before him, he came to the throne when he was too young to know how to be an effective leader. Even if he had been taught, the consensus seems to be that he still would not have effectively acted in his position.

While Rome saw a number of weak rulers come and go, Honorius went down as the worst of the lot. His failure to grasp the situation and respond cost Rome its final glory. During his time, he allowed the city to be completely overrun, doing nothing to stop the last vestige of a once distinguished and powerful nation from being ravaged and ruined.

Only a Child

Born to Theodosius I in 384 CE, he was named co-ruler while still a young boy because his father was facing threats and pressure from those trying to usurp the throne (Cavazzi, 2021). Having survived a few civil wars and a long-term illness, the need for an heir was apparent. Two years later, the emperor died and a young Honorius, only ten years old, was suddenly ruler.

Realizing the task of managing all of Rome was too difficult, it was split between him and his brother. He became emperor of Western Rome, while Arcadius, his sibling, took over the eastern section.

Further intervention was needed to ensure stability in the empire, and General Stilicho was appointed overseer. A very competent military leader who had served under Theodosius, Stilicho now became Hoinorius' trusted advisor, although most of the decisions during the early years came from him. To solidify the relationship, Honorius married Stilicho's daughter.

Defending Attacks

Instead of remaining in Rome, the capital was moved to Ravenna. It was ideal in terms of protection because of its robust fortifications, but also due to a long string of marshes that made attack very difficult. It was easy to defend but made it very difficult to also protect the city of Rome, which lay vulnerable and open to attack.

While Stilicho remained, any attack or revolt was subdued. Honorius had little to do during this period but relied on his general to keep the peace. The military was kept busy in North Africa putting down an uprising and then had to rush back as the Visigoths entered Italy under the command of a king named Alaric. The Roman forces of Britain and Gaul were ordered to come and assist, and, after a number of skirmishes, Stilicho saw the invaders off.

When Alaric tried again, instead of fighting him off, Stilicho bribed him to cease his advances. The general forced the Senate to cough up 4,000 pounds of gold, which was paid to the invader (Cavazzi, 2021). Many of the officials in Rome were incensed by the move, and, since Stilicho was half-Vandal, half-Roman, they suspected collusion between him and Alaric.

No More Direction

Stilicho's movements around Constantinople continued to bother the Senate as they worried he was making gains for selfish reasons. Hostilities between East and West were at an all-time high, and outlying provinces continued to fall. When his daughter died, Stilicho organized another marriage between his other daughter and Honorius.

While the general was away defending the empire, Honorius was listening to Olympius, a minister who fed him stories of how Stilicho was taking over. He persuaded the young man to believe that his trusted military advisor, who had done everything to protect his empire, was now conspiring with the Barbarians to overthrow the emperor. No sooner had Stilicho returned from battle, than he was arrested and executed.

Loyal supporters of Stilicho were rounded up and tortured or killed. In an attempt to put down any further supposed conspiracies, Honorius had everyone close to his former advisor dealt with. Officials, family members, and troops were targeted. Stilicho's daughter was exiled, his son killed, and any family members of those serving under the general were massacred. The result was a massive defection of soldiers over to Alaric.

No Answers

Without the strong guidance and protection of his trusted military overseer, Honorius was lost. Having made no real decisions of his own up to that point, he now faced a crumbling empire and an invasion that he had no answers for.

Frequent skirmishes had been taking place along the borders of Rome, eating away at the edges of Honorius' empire. Without a strong leader, he had no one to turn to and no one to rely on to keep the invaders at bay. It was only a matter of time before they set their eyes on Rome, open and unprotected.

A few years after Stilicho was killed, Gaul and Britain were attacked, but this time Honorius refused to get involved, even though they had rushed to his aid before. He chose to leave them to their own. Known as the *Rescript of Honorius,* letters were sent out to the governors instructing them that no help would come and that they needed to defend themselves (Hudson, 2016). By this time, the empire saw numerous attacks across its borders, and the emperor was unable or unwilling to do much about it.

Alaric, who had been forced back by Stilicho before, once again marched into Italy demanding land and money owed to him. Honorius stalled until it was almost too late. With the enemy camped outside, besieging the city, and famine on the doorstep, the emperor was more worried about money than the people. In the end, he reluctantly paid over the gold and silver, ending the blockade.

With the Visigoths still within the borders, a tenuous peace negotiation began, but again Honorius could not make up his mind. When it looked like a settlement could be reached, Honorius pulled out, angering Alaric.

Chicken or City

On 24 August 410 CE, the city of Rome was attacked (Cavazzi, 2021). There was hardly any defensive measure from Honorius, who sat at his new capital, Ravenna, and waited while the Visigoths took over. For three days, the enemy sacked Rome with no countermeasure from the emperor.

A story written around this time by Procopius to demonstrate the incompetence of this young ruler.

Honorius loved feathered animals: the more stunning the plumage, the better the bird. Pigeons and chickens were his favorite, especially one rooster he aptly named Roma. Instead of dealing with issues of impending attacks and rebellions in the provinces, the emperor would pay all his attention to looking after Roma and the other poultry.

During the attack on the city, Honorius was calmly sitting in his room when a servant burst claiming "Rome has perished!" The ruler was visibly shocked. He went pale and could not find his breath as the news hit home. With an ashen face, Honorius shook his head and replied, "But it has just taken food from my hand!" The servant realized the confusion and told Honorius that it was the city, not the bird that had fallen, to which the ruler quickly added "I feared that it was my beloved rooster that had perished" (Jesse, 2015).

A rooster

While it may have a touch of fiction in it, the story sums up Honorius' inability to act when the empire's most prized possession was taken. While little damage was done physically to buildings and people, the honor and glory of a mighty kingdom were tarnished and would never rise again.

Ruined Reputation

With the city having fallen, Honorius' standing as emperor was never the same. He suffered a number of setbacks, even after Alaric died. Many usurpers popped up, declaring they were now the ruler. Instead of decisive victories, Honorius was forced to settle treaties and appease those who were looking to carve large portions of the empire for themselves.

Another general was given the dirty work of trying to maintain the nation's borders, and, if it had not been for Constantius, Honorius' reign would have probably ended much sooner. In the end, he died of a similar illness to what befell his father. Making very little impact on the timeline or the territory, his moment as emperor is mainly remembered for being the one in charge while Rome was sacked!

Chapter 8:

Sabotage and Conspiracy in the Roman Empire

A nation can survive its fools, and even the ambitious. But it cannot survive treason from within. An enemy at the gates is less formidable, for he is known and carries his banner openly. But the traitor moves amongst those within the gate freely, his sly whispers rustling through all the alleys, heard in the very halls of government itself.
–Cicero

Where there is power, there are men and women hungry for it. They set their eyes on it and become consumed with attaining what is only available to a few. The fight for top spot, for control and authority over others, can be outright fierce, ending in bloodshed, or it can be subversive like snakes in the grass.

With the office of the emperor, there was untold power that stretched as far as the boundaries of Rome, including every person within that vast empire. It included thousands of soldiers ready to spring into action and defend the nation. Countless wealth and benefits came with the job. There was also the promise of being exalted onto every stone pedestal, chiseled into history for generations to come.

It is no surprise that with the power of being a ruler in Rome, there was also the constant menace of those who wanted to take it for themselves. Almost every emperor was either caught in the midst of schemes to bring them down or spent lots of time trying to put the fires of treason out.

Some of these threats came from close colleagues, even family members, while others rose with men who looked to extend their growing base of support. There were subtle whispers of conspiracies involving attempted murder and poison. There were loud accusations that led to war. Some emperors survived, others did not.

These are some of the stories of the sabotage and subterfuge that these emperors had to face.

Julius Caesar

One of the most famous statesmen, he was far ahead of his time. Caesar led his army to incredible victories and, in doing so, became more powerful than the senators. This threatened everything they believed Rome was about, as having a dictator call the shots went against the fabric of the Republic.

Had Caesar lived to transform Rome, he would have been the first emperor, but the men who stood beside him, like Brutus, plunged daggers into his back. While they assumed they were acting on behalf of the people, when the population heard of the death, instead of cheering, they cried and howled.

It was a warning for all those to come: who would fill the shoes of reigning over such a fickle and untrustworthy government in which trust only went so far?

Statue of Julius Caesar

Augustus

The first emperor was, in comparison to the majority of rulers that came later, worthy of his place in the palace. He brought about change while still keeping the Senate intact, even if it had far less clout than before. But he was not safe from those who wanted to oust him and take his place or return Rome back to being a republic.

Marcus Lepidus the Younger was the son of Julius Caesar's commander and was himself a senator. In 30 BCE, plans to kill Agustus when he returned to the city after defeating his rivals were uncovered with Lepidus at the very center of the plot. He was swiftly executed, and, when his wife, Serwilla heard about it, swallowed hot coals to kill herself (Jasinski, 2021a).

Another uprising involved Egnatius Rufus, who formed a gang under the disguise of being the fire brigade. When he applied for consul but was denied, his thugs took to the streets where they clashed with officials. Drumming up support from the civilians, Rufus' uprising threatened to overwhelm the city. Augustus returned in time and ordered the upstart to be caught and killed for causing dangerous public disorder.

Tiberius

Sejanus had everything he needed to topple the emperor. He had the command of soldiers, he was running the city, and he was trusted by Tiberius. His takeover almost worked.

As Praetorian Prefect, he began consolidating the scattered garrisons into one place and stepped up the number of cohorts to twelve, with one permanently in the palace. On top of this, he unified the unit into 12,000 men that were completely under his authority.

Even though he had the force to engineer a coup, he did not abuse his power at this point, as he was content to remain at the emperor's side. Tiberius called him "*Socius Laborum*" (my partner in hardships), and he was loyal to the emperor (Jasinski, 2021a). A monument was built in his honor at Pompeii's Theater, and he enjoyed the command and authority of his position in the city. But others in the Senate and the imperial family felt threatened, especially Tiberius' son, Drusus.

Sejanus, realizing his position had become precarious, had Drusus slowly poisoned over time so it would look as though he was just getting sick until he died a "natural" death. By this time Tiberius had become paranoid and moved to Capri in 26 CE (Jasinski, 2021a). Deeming his other eleven villas not defensible or worthy as an emperor's abode, he built Villa Jovis on a mountaintop, with steep cliffs and harsh terrain surrounding it. The largest of his residences, it had a spectacular view across the ocean.

Rome, in his absence, was left in the care of his right-hand man, Sejanus, who did just that. All correspondence between Rome and the island of Capri was carefully monitored so Sejanus could control what the emperor knew and what he did not. Sejanus' birthday became a public festival, and statues were erected in his honor. While exalting his name across the capital, he had been hard at work removing any trace of opposition.

When the time was finally right, Sejanus began to plan his coup. His only problem was Antonio the Younger, a man loyal to the emperor, who got wind of the impending overthrow. Warning Tiberius just in time, the absent ruler ordered Macron to take matters into his hands and seize Sejanus. He was caught and summarily executed.

Caligula

Although this account of betrayal has already been mentioned, it is worth describing the extent of conspiracies and the effect they have on an emperor. Having grown up in Tiberius' household, where there was a constant state of paranoia, Caligula was no stranger to threats, real or false.

His own sisters, Livilla and Agrippina the Younger (Nero's mother), rose up against him, conspiring to get rid of him. Livilla's husband, Aemilius Lepidus, was executed for his part in it, but the two women were exiled to the Pontine islands. Instead of execution, banishment was standard practice in this regard, especially when it came to family members.

This was not the only plot, and Caligula went on a rampage to root out any and every threat to his life. If it was just a word spoken against him, he executed that person! His ruthlessness went so far as to order the father of one of the prisoners he was going to execute, to watch the ordeal (Jasinski, 2021a). Just as Tiberius had done, he tried to wipe out all possible enemies with an iron fist.

Claudius

Claudius was not a very strong leader. His frailty made him a target for anyone looking to steal his place, but he seems to have had some luck on his side (or fate!). In 42 CE, a senator named Lucius Annius Vinicianus sought to drive Cladius from the palace and began gathering supporters, one of them being Camillus (Jasinski, 2021a). Loyal to the cause, Camillus was in charge of a number of legions.

With this show of force, Lucius made his intentions public: he wanted to restore power to the Senate. When the emperor heard this, he was ready to surrender without a fight and relinquish his post to the general. Everything was in Camillus' favor except for fate.

His soldiers refused to move and rebelled against him. That morning, the men struggled to decorate the legionary eagles and could not raise them off the ground. This was a very bad omen, and, for such a superstitious nation, they were not going to test fate. In the end, the traitor Camillus fled and committed suicide.

But the worst was yet to come for Claudius. His beloved wife, Messalina, was named as part of a conspiracy to kill the emperor. Although she was known to be extremely promiscuous and even left him to marry another man, he still loved her and always believed she was innocent of the charges. Nevertheless, she was executed.

Nero

Lucius Calpurnius Piso got in with the wrong crowd.

As a politician and orator, he was very well-known and very well-liked throughout the city. People used to flock to hear him speak in the courts, and it helped that he was good-looking and had an affable character. He had no ties to the Julio-Claudian dynasty, and so had absolutely no claim to the throne. As a senator, he held enough sway with the officials, but not too much that Nero needed to be alarmed or worried.

However, when he joined with others like himself, the group as a collective garnered much support and a significant amount of power. His allies included men from the Senate, the equestrian circles, as well as the Praetorian Guard.

When Nero discovered the existence of this band of men that was plotting against him, he sentenced 19 to death and exiled 13 more (Jasinski, 2021a). Seneca, Nero's former tutor, and the poet, Gaius Petronius, were among those who died as a result.

The Year of Four Emperors

69 C.E. was one of the most tumultuous periods in Roman history. The end of Nero resulted in near-anarchy as prominent men vied for the empty throne. The previous year had seen a universal cry for the emperor's rule to come to an end. Nero was so despised that a group of conspirators began organizing a rebellion. At the center of these plans was a governor named Vindex. With the support of Galba, a man who had served dutifully under both Caligula and Nero, Vindex declared himself emperor but failed to make any headway in his cause when he lost the Battle of Vesontio (Vermeulen, 2020).

By this time, Nero's mercurial moods saw more politicians openly throwing their lot behind Galba, with the emperor's own Praetorian Guard switching sides. Nero fled in terror and ended up slashing his throat in fear for his life. The sudden vacuum of power led to a scramble that saw four men fill the role of ruler in as little as a year.

Galba, an established leader of the revolt, was quickly endorsed by the Senate as their choice, despite his reputation of being greedy and cruel. When he finally arrived in Rome to assume his position, many regretted their decision. Property was seized, taxes were raised, and anyone suspicious of dissent was executed. Two of Galba's henchmen were honored instead of held accountable for their corrupt dealings. Worst of all, the new ruler refused to pay the legions what they were owed.

The growing tide of discontent saw another general, Aulus Vitellius, being put forward as emperor by his soldiers in Germania. Meanwhile, Galba was murdered by his own Praetorian Guard. On 15 January, his body was dumped in the street (Vermeulen, 2020). His head was delivered to another senator, Marcus Salvius Otho, who had the backing of the Senate and became the next official Roman potentate.

However, Vitellius was not about to give up his rightful place in the palace and continued to march with his troops into Rome, ignoring offers of a peace settlement with Otho. The ensuing war began successfully for Otho with three small victories, but he suffered a major setback at the Battle of Bedriacum where 40,000 Romans died (Vermeulen, 2020). Otho, overcome that his hand was responsible for so many deaths, shared his money and said farewell before committing suicide. Having only served in the post of emperor for three months, his short rule had an impact on those nearest to him as "many of the soldiers who were present kissed his hands and feet as he lay dead, weeping bitterly and calling him the bravest of men and an incomparable emperor" (Vermeulen, 2020).

With another leader dead, the Senate did an about-turn and threw its support behind the warlord, Vitellius, who was slowly making his way back to Rome. It was more like a celebratory sojourn as he partied and feasted in every city along the way, his soldiers having free reign to do as they pleased.

On reaching Bedriacum, the men were shocked at the rotting corpses still strewn across the battlefield. Even more appalling was Vitellius' response to seeing the thousands of dead bodies: "The odor of a dead enemy was sweet and that of a fellow citizen sweeter still" (Vermeulen,

2020). His cruelty followed him all the way back to the capital where he paid homage to none other than Nero!

He ruled for eight months until Vespasian entered the scene, challenging Vitellius' position by being declared emperor by his own forces. With growing support, Vespasian's forces aimed for Rome, sweeping through with victory after victory. The hardest battle would again be at Bedriacum, but instead of might, it would be decided by misunderstanding. Having picked up the custom of saluting the sun from their days in Syria, Vespasian's soldiers were seen doing this the morning after a hard night of fighting. The enemy thought they were saluting reinforcements, and so fled.

Bust of Vespasian

They would continue running until Rome, where the battle became fierce and scrappy. Vitellius' men threw roof tiles at opponents and trapped them in winding streets, but they were outnumbered. Vitellius disguised himself in rags to escape; however, he was caught and dragged by a noose to the center where he was tortured before being decapitated. On 22 December, Vespasian became the fourth emperor to rule Rome (Vermeulen, 2020).

Proving to be a competent candidate, Vespasian ruled as emperor for 10 years, setting up the Flavian Dynasty.

Titus

Terentius Maximus was a doppelganger for Nero. He was the perfect substitute in appearance and behavior, being able to sing and play the lyre as well. Using this "gift," he began building a base of support as the emperor in the outlying provinces, dismissing reports of his death as fake news. This pretender approached the Party and began amassing a following, causing a "Nero revival." Terentius 'biggest con was persuading King Artabanus III of the Parthians to honor his debt of having Armenia returned to him (Jasinski, 2021a). He also held ill-will toward Titus, who had taken over as emperor.

The king initially fell for it and made plans to restore Nero to his rightful place on the Roman throne. But somehow, he was alerted to the ruse and instead of crowning Terentius with a laurel wreath, had him executed.

He was not the only look-alike; two other claims to the throne were made by Nero after his death, one 20 years later during Domitian's reign!

Domitian

Some attempts were not so subtle, and a civil war broke out in 89 CE, with Lucius Antony declaring himself emperor instead of Domitian (Jasinski 2021a). A senator and commander, he initiated a rebellion in Upper Germania with plans to amalgamate forces with his allies there. These reinforcements never arrived because the ice on the Rhine had melted, making it impossible for them to cross and join their compatriots. Outnumbered and with their main force stuck on the other side, the rebellion was quickly crushed. Interestingly, the leader of the troops sent to quell the uprising was none other than Trajan, the future emperor.

After this, Domitian feared for his life more than ever, and the end of his reign saw him clamp down on the slightest threat with excessive and overt harshness.

Marcus Aurelius

Avidius Cassius has the fame of being part of an attempt at taking the throne that failed due to bad timing. He had been ready to jump into action and take his place as emperor: plans had already been in motion for anyone to become ruler other than Commodus. Marcus Aurelius ' wife was at the heart of the conspiracy, ensuring that a capable candidate like Cassius would be able to deny her son his rightful position.

The problem was that Cassius jumped into action too soon. Hearing false reports of the emperor's death, he rushed in and declared himself as sovereign leader over Rome, claiming his legionaries had elected him. When Cassius realized the news he had been fed was not true, and that Marcus Aurelius 'troops far outnumbered the rebel forces he had, things turned on the usurper. His own centurion and decurion decided it was not a battle they wanted to fight and killed Cassius, sending his head to the real emperor as proof of their loyalty.

Maximinus Thrax

Sometimes, names were thrown into the running for the top spot without their consent. A senator and friend of the murdered Alexander Severus, Quartinus was also the commander of a contingent of archers. Without agreeing to it, his men proclaimed him emperor because they did not agree with Maximinus Trax's role in the killing of his predecessor. In the end, Quartinus, the reluctant candidate, was betrayed and killed by his own soldiers.

Claudius II

Appius Claudius Censorinus was a mistake! An example of soldiers putting someone up for the job only to regret the decision later,

Censorinus was not exactly what they had hoped for in a leader. In a bid to put someone else in the place of the ruling Claudius II, the troops elected their own commander as emperor in 269 CE (Jasinski, 2021a). He never caused any real threat to Rome or Claudius II because his own men killed him a few days after putting his name forward. It turned out that Censorinus was so strict, the soldiers could not handle his extreme discipline, so they backed down on their rebellion and took the commander out.

Aurelian

One way to topple the government is through economic turmoil. Felicissimus was an imperial official overseeing the state treasury. Getting the slaves who worked at the royal mint on his side, he was going to flood the market with counterfeit coins. The financial crisis would have been enough to bring about a revolution. The plot was uncovered before any fake money could be released and Felicissimus was killed.

In the end, the scheme resulted in 7,000 soldiers being killed and a number of senators getting sentenced to death (Jasinski, 2021a). Rather than a small inside job, it turned out to be a larger, more concerted effort at overthrowing the emperor.

Chapter 9:

Lust and Scandal at the Imperial Court

I came, I saw, I conquered.
–Julius Caesar

Scandals attach themselves to almost every emperor, regardless of how well they conducted their time on the throne. Even the revered rulers have skeletons in the closet that historians love to rattle and display, even if they might be more fiction than fact. When it comes to sex, Rome was a hotbed for fun, experimentation, and immorality. Some rulers were open to anything, with anyone!

Nero and Caligula have become infamous for their abuse of civility, going so far as public consummation. Elagabalus pushed the boundaries even further, keeping everyone guessing which side of the fence he was on. While they stole the limelight for frolicking around, there were scores of others who imbibed the heady juices of shameful sexuality.

Condoned

However, rather than being a completely promiscuous culture, Rome actually abided by a set of standards and rules. Often lauded as a logical and ordered people, there was a modicum of decency that held the fabric of their society from completely splitting at the seams and tumbling into a mass of degenerate iniquity.

Mos maiorum (the way of the elders) was the customary code of conduct for moral behavior, including sexual practice (Ricketts, 2021). Although unwritten, they defined what was acceptable and what was not, drawing a line against sexual excess that went beyond normal self-control. There were written laws added to this general consensus surrounding intercourse, outlawing rape, and other offenses. This, however, did not extend to those of the lower class, like prostitutes and performers, and violating a slave was seen more as property damage against the owner than a rape case against the servant.

Largely a male-dominated society, women were expected to be subservient, marrying for practicality and not pleasure. Infidelity on the part of men was common, and a wife was required to overlook such instances as long as it involved an unmarried woman or a boy who was of age. So, when it came to Julius Caesar taking Cleopatra as a lover, it was not adulterous because she was not a Roman citizen (Ricketts, 2021).

Homosexuality was tolerated if it was by consent. Even in this, male dominance was at play since a man who was submissive in the relationship was disregarded as being a real man. Effeminacy was not acceptable and was only for slaves, servants, or prostitutes. Other than that, it was widely practiced in a similar fashion to ancient Greece where the male body was something to be praised, adored, and enjoyed.

It's understandable that freedom of sexuality existed during this period since the religious order of the day promoted it in its statues, doctrine, and rituals. Temple prostitution was a very common rite, unless a woman was a Vestal Virgin, which meant they were celibate and off-limits. The literature and art of the day speak of a society that did not shun intercourse but embraced it, so long as it did not cross moral boundaries.

Statue of Hemaphrodite

Yet, what happened behind closed doors and in the shadows was not always proper. Scandalous affairs were often the talk of the city, especially when it came to high-ranking officials, even the emperors!

Escapades

Julius Caesar

Some historians refute this account of Caesar's early days before he became ruler, but jokes and teasing about the incident continued throughout his life, so some of it may be true. Nevertheless, like most Roman scandals, it is spicy even when taken with a pinch of salt.

Twenty years old and handsome, Caesar was serving in Asia Minor under Lucius Lucullus in 80 BCE when he was required to visit the king of Bithynia, Nicomedes IV (Jasinski, 2021b). His task in the royal court was to convince the monarch to send his fleet to assist in the siege that was taking place on the island of Lesbos. Caesar did his job so well that Nicomedes took a liking to the young soldier, keeping him in the palace for longer than necessary.

The oriental lifestyle and architecture were spellbinding, as was the lifestyle of those who lived in the royal residence. Intoxicated by his experiences, Caesar became Nicomedes 'lover. Romans would never have blinked an eye at the relationship, except for the rumors that the king was the dominant partner and not Caesar. The young man was even caught wearing a woman's outfit, meaning he played the passive role. This behavior was not condoned back in Rome, even receiving the death penalty on certain occasions. Caesar's biggest punishment for his Bithynian romp was to have to put up with a slew of tasteless banter that followed him into his days as emperor.

Cleopatra

The famed Queen of the Nile got her claws into not one, but two rulers. Her charm and guile were so potent that she managed to seduce her way into keeping her throne and sharing power with Rome's elite.

When Caesar defeated Pompey in 48 BCE, he became the master of the Roman world. The Egyptian needed a way to bolster her waning power so she could rebuild what was left of her empire. She set her sights on the new leader, and, as fate would have it, he was on a state visit in Alexandria. Her only problem was she had been banished from the city by her brother. Not one to pass up an opportunity, she snuck into Caesar's room in a daring plan. As Plutarch (Mark, 2018) writes:

> So Cleopatra, taking only Apollodorus the Sicilian from among her friends, embarked in a little skiff and landed at the palace when it was already getting dark; and as it was impossible to escape notice otherwise, she stretched herself at full length inside a bed-sack, while Apollodorus tied the bed-sack up with a cord and carried it indoors to Caesar. It was by this device of Cleopatra's, it is said, that Caesar was first captivated, for she showed herself to be a bold coquette, and succumbing to the charm of further intercourse with her, he reconciled her to her

brother on the basis of a joint share with him in the royal power. (para. 1)

A family feud followed when Cleopatra's brother got wind of the ruse, but with Caesar's troops in play, this was quickly ended. The queen was restored to power and, for a time, remained the emperor's mistress. Both she and her lover spent much time on Nile cruises, touring the desert kingdom. It was the perfect combination of business and pleasure.

Things became complicated when the Egyptian queen bore Caesar a son, something his own wife back in Rome had not been able to do up to this point. The boy was named Caesarion and was given a future claim to his father's inheritance. To make matters worse, the Roman emperor was so enamored with his new exotic family that he brought them on a visit to the capital city.

Although they were welcomed, the Senate was affronted and incensed, and plans were set in motion for what would become one of the most famous assassinations in history.

Antony

Cleopatra fled Rome with her son after the death of her lover. However, Marc Antony, a good friend of Caesar's and a newly appointed leader along with Octavian, wanted answers. He summoned the queen to Tarsus to clear her name of being involved in the assassination plot. Instead of rushing, she purposefully delayed arriving, and, when she finally did, managed to catch her second Roman ruler. Plutarch (Mark, 2018) sets the scene:

> She came sailing up the river Cydnus in a barge with gilded stern and outspread sails of purple, while oars of silver beat time to the music of flutes and fifes and harps. She herself lay all along, under a canopy of cloth of gold, dressed as Venus in a picture, and beautiful young boys, like painted Cupids, stood on each side to fan her. Her maids were dressed like Sea Nymphs and Graces, some steering at the rudder, some working at the ropes...perfumes diffused themselves from the vessel to the

shore, which was covered with multitudes, part following the galley up the river on either bank, part running out of the city to see the sight. The market place was quite emptied, and Antony at last was left alone sitting upon the tribunal while the word went, through all the multitude, that Venus was come to feast with Bacchus for the common good of Asia.

Instead of interrogation, he ended up consoling and comforting the "grieving" queen. Still married to Octavia back in Rome, Antony set off on an affair that would last 10 years and bear him children. Eventually, he divorced his Roman wife so that he could legally marry his true love.

But the Senate had had enough of the meddling seductress, especially Octavian, whose sister, Octavia, had just been jilted by Antony as a result of her wiles. Turning on his co-leader, Octavian marched on Egypt. The end of the couple is a tragic tale reminiscent of Romeo and Juliet. Antony heard a rumor that Cleopatra had died, and so stabbed himself. Meanwhile, left on her own, with Octavian close by, she took her own life by the poison of a snake.

Julia

Augustus may have been rated one of the finest emperors in terms of political stability during the shift from Republic to Empire. Maintaining the Senate's place in society, even though it had lost most of its power, was a big feat. While he hardly features on any lists of Roman infamy or scandal, one of his family members does make an appearance.

Julia, his daughter, was given everything an aristocratic girl needed for her status. She grew up under Augustus' watchful eye, not being allowed to talk to anyone who was not first screened and permitted by him. He loved her but had a tough time keeping her under control.

Initially set up to marry Marc Antony's son, this union never came as a result of the civil war and fallout between the two rulers. At the age of 14, she married her cousin, then at 18 was wedded to one of the emperor's generals. When he died, she married the up-and-coming heir to the throne, Tiberius, in 11 BCE (Jasinski, 2021b). This was common practice among imperial dynasties to ensure power remained in the family.

Whether it was her strict upbringing, being married at such an early age, or an innate sexual drive, Julia slipped out and visited numerous other men's beds. This behavior began during her second marriage and lasted up until Augustus stepped in and filed divorce papers on behalf of her third husband. Tiberius, at this stage, was holed up on the island of Rhodes, probably ashamed and embarrassed by his wife's shenanigans.

Her string of lovers included men from many of the top Roman families, which caused even more of a stir, since Augustus was desperately trying to reinstate good ethics into society. While he championed the cause of moral reform, she undid it all as she hopped from bed to bed. She was eventually exiled, where she died from being starved under Tiberius' orders.

Tiberius

Ironically, Julia's embarrassed husband makes this list, as well. It was typical of many emperors, who often denounced other people's actions while they themselves behaved far worse.

Having removed himself from public, the emperor moved to the island of Capri where he spent his last days. Having delegated all official duties to Sejanus, Tiberius focused on gratifying his sexual pleasures. After much effort, he managed to accumulate one of the largest collections of erotic books, pornographic paintings, and lewd sculptures (Jasinski, 2021b). When he was offered a choice between a large sum of money or a painting depicting mythical lovers, he opted for the latter, hanging it in his bedroom.

With all this literature and art to fuel his libido, Tiberius also gathered a sizeable contingent of boys and girls, who were purely there for his pleasure. Besides enjoying watching others in the act of intercourse, he often joined in, apparently inventing a threesome that involved only men (Jasinski, 2021b). Any visitors to the island were either invited or forced to join in, with severe consequences if they refused.

But it is the accounts of "games" that were set up around the island, some in the forest, others in the water, that really show the reclusive emperor's depravity. He would hunt children in the woods at night, and, if he caught any of them, he had his way with them. He is reported to have taught boys to play "fish" where they dived under the water, using their teeth and lips to tease and please the emperor (Jasinski, 2021b).

Bust of Tiberius

The history of this island reads like the diary of a bored, sick-minded pedophile.

Caligula

This emperor's notoriety is mostly because of his cruelty and twisted sense of humor. Apart from bedding his own sisters, he was known to associate with married women, even with their husbands aware of what was going on. He often whispered in women's ears as he was caressing them that with just one word, he could have that beautiful neck that he was kissing cut for his own pleasure (Aldrete, 2019).

Caligula would kidnap women during feasts, have his way with them, and return them to the banquet where they would act as if nothing happened. One such incident was less subtle: the emperor took Gaius Piso's new wife to his own chambers after the wedding ceremony, bringing her back a while later with the claim that he had done just as Romulus had when snatching the Sabine women for Rome (Jasinski, 2021b).

His own marriages lasted only as long as he was pleasured, and he divorced Livia when he discovered another beautiful lady. Caligula was so enchanted by Lolia Paulina that he ordered her to be brought to Rome where he commanded her to divorce her husband and marry him. They were together for a few weeks before the emperor annulled the marriage and forbade her from sexual contact with any other men. He soon found another wife in the form of a baker's daughter.

Stories of homosexuality followed him all through his reign, which is ironic because the man who led the charge to unseat him from the throne was a senator whom Caligula mocked for being effeminate and having a high-pitched voice.

Messalina

One of the most notorious women in Roman history, Messalina was the third wife of Emperor Claudius. He loved her and found it difficult to order her execution when she decided to marry another senator even though she was still married to the emperor. Although he still thought of her as "submissive," to the rest of Rome, she was renowned as having been a nymphomaniac and involved in numerous orgies (Jasinski, 2021b). Her most scandalous feat was to challenge a professional prostitute in a bet over who could bed the most men in a single night. Messalina tallied up an impressive score of 150, winning the endurance contest.

Sporus

Sporus was a slave who reminded Nero of his wife, Poppea (whom he killed after kicking her pregnant belly). As a result of his looks, he was brought into the palace and, on the emperor's orders, had to undergo castration (Jasinski, 2021b). It was not the only change: Sporus became Sabina as part of his sex change.

Forced to wear women's clothing, be involved in girlish activities, and always surrounded by ladies, he was deemed a female. But Nero was not happy and offered large sums to anyone who could complete the task of making Sporus into a complete physical woman.

On Nero's year-long trip to Greece in 66 CE, he engaged in a full wedding ceremony to Sporus, although this was never ratified back in Rome (Jasinski, 2021b). The ex-slave, now turned woman, stayed by his lover's side until the very end. But, in the final days when Nero, cowering in his villa outside Rome, demanded that they both commit suicide together, Sporus took off.

Elagabalus

The list would not be complete without mentioning the young bisexual emperor again. His florid antics were headliners for every gossipmonger, taking the Roman scandal ratings to a new high. Even though the nation allowed for the odd dalliance or delinquency, his bisexual tendencies tested the veneer of moral fabric that held the empire together.

His relationship with the charioteer, Hierocles, has already been told, but an interesting side note of the story is how Elagabalus found his long-time partner. Servants routinely visited baths and other establishments, seeking anybody who stood out in terms of being well-endowed. Hierocles, however, literally fell at the emperor's feet.

Seated in the imperial box, watching the games, Elagabalus got a pleasant surprise when one of the chariots tipped, sending its driver flying off. The young man fell in front of the royal entourage, his helmet coming off to reveal an exquisite shock of blonde hair. Elagabalus jumped to his feet at the sight, his heart a flutter in lust. Hierocles immediately found himself whisked off to the palace where he was showered with gifts and all of the emperor's adoration and attention.

Elagabalus made no secret of his relationship, saying "I am glad to be called mistress, consort, queen of Hierocles" (Jasinski, 2021b).

Conclusion

History is never black and white. While facts are stacked together to form the basis of what took place, it is never solely monochromatic because it is written by people about people. Any time men and women are involved, there is emotion, opinion, and character. These are never black and white, they are multicolor. For all its facts and figures, history is also filled in with shades and tones of humanity.

In many narratives, the glory of Rome is often washed in a gloss of shimmering resplendence. Standing out as one of the pinnacles of history, it shone brightly in its heyday of politics, power, and principle. For hundreds of years, the empire stood as a testimony to mankind's ability to harness the best that humanity has to offer and flourish. Each victory is gilded in triumphant glows.

But there are more colors teeming deep beneath this shining veneer. Below the sheen of wonder, there are other hues historians have used to recreate the events thousands of years ago. Each fact is served up with a generous stroke of description and interpretation. Shocking and explicit at times, it is as much a portrayal of Rome in its fullness. Removing the golden tinge, it becomes clear that two other shades of historical color bring the Roman era to life. In this light, accounts of the empire reveal stark contrasts.

One side has dark, rough brushstrokes of wars, military campaigns, and gladiator fights. Sprays of bright red are mixed with somber, smokey black that spreads ominously across many deadly battlefields all the way to the gritty arena of the Colosseum. Graphically violent, the days of emperors were seldom without the glint of blood-tipped spears and swords.

There is another palette used to render the ancient days of Rome. A fleshy pink with lusty overtones of bedroom antics and writhing bodies. A collection of sordid depictions underlies almost every ruler's reign, often leaning sensually toward depraved and debauched. Enough to raise eyebrows, the stories have become legendary showers of pastel pornography as emperors cross-dressed, reveled in orgies, and found inventive ways to release their urges.

The accounts of the emperors rest mainly on the prolific artwork of a few biographers of that day: Seutonius, Cassius Dio, Tacitus, and Herodian (with a few others added in for extra color). While claiming to be black and white, based in fact, and using an unbiased quill to depict the rulers and their lives, modern experts are not all in agreement with this.

When it comes to the chronicles of Nero, Caligula, Domitian, Commodus, Elagabalus, and Honorius, the versions of these reigns are often exceedingly exuberant in detail, their brushes dipped heavily in storytelling to paint the Roman Empire under such emperors in a crude, violent, and licentious light. With the Senate enforcing a moratorium to remove and defame such emperors, there is a good chance that the historians (of which a few were senators or held some political post themselves) used a prejudiced palette to further shame them.

Cassius Dio, who wrote one of the only surviving texts about some of the initial emperors, had a public dislike for certain rulers, especially Commodus (Roos, 2021). Much of his writing is tainted with a tinge of personal distaste, which brings the veracity of his work into question. Suetonius had a similar penchant for dipping his historical pen into the pot of poetic license. Tacitus, too, mixed colors when it came to producing his annals of Roman history. In addition, inconsistencies and dubious evidence can be discerned when under a microscope.

These accounts cannot be disregarded because they have a few embellishments, since they form the main body of work pertaining to these emperors (there are not enough surviving documents to properly refute all they say). If the historians of the day used very broad, liberal brushstrokes to illustrate their stories, then black and white they are not. Each must be read with a certain skepticism just as an examiner would view a painting. Instead of taking every story at face value, a keen eye is required to see beyond the spurious smears. As with any good story, there is legend and there is gospel.

Nero playing the fiddle while Rome burns may be a flagrant splash of propaganda. Caligula's bedroom antics with his sisters could be a desperate attempt to discredit him. Honorius and his rooster is most probably more of a bedtime story than historical fact. But these emperors do not escape the bad rap they get because of some extra color added to their narratives.

Strip away the blatant brushstrokes, peel back the layers of political mud that have been slung at these men, and a picture still remains. There are enough lines that can be connected to still show these emperors as far from being above reproach. With nothing to hide behind but the stark black-and-white outlines, each emperor remains cast in infamy.

Nero persecuted the Christians with atrocious methods—that is well documented. Elagabalus did have relations with men. Commodus did spend more time in the ring than on the throne—there are enough facts to make a movie about it. Domitian ruled with a severity that saw many being purged and killed under his rule—no contest to that. If only for the hard, naked truth, then these men deserve their portraits in the hall of shame.

While there may be other Roman rulers who enjoyed the sight of blood, ran around the palace with no clothes on, or saw themselves as more than human, these few went outside of the lines. They broke moral borders in a rush toward depravity and insanity. These infamous emperors were the dark blots on the golden era of Rome. To fully appreciate their notoriety, their sordid tales are worth reading in full three-dimensional, polychromatic color!

References

Aldrete, G. (2019, December 9). *Caligula: The embodiment of cruelty.* Wondrium Daily. https://www.wondriumdaily.com/caligula-the-embodiment-of-cruelty/

Bernett, R. (2020, August). *The crisis of the third century: The reign of Elagabalus.* Wondrium Daily. https://www.wondriumdaily.com/the-crisis-of-the-third-century-the-reign-of-elagabalus/

Bileta, V. (2020, May 1). *Caligula: 18 Facts on the "mad" Roman emperor.* TheCollector. https://www.thecollector.com/caligula/

Bileta, V. (2023, February). *5 myths about Emperor Nero you need to stop believing.* TheCollector. https://www.thecollector.com/roman-emperor-nero-myths/

Bledsoe, E. (2023, October 2). *What military leader said I came, I saw, I conquered?* The Soldiers Project. https://www.thesoldiersproject.org/what-military-leader-said-i-came-i-saw-i-conquered/

Catalano, J. (2000, May). *History reveals a truly nasty emperor—and he wasn't much of a gladiator, either.* Los Angeles Times. https://www.latimes.com/archives/la-xpm-2000-may-10-ca-28341-story.html

Cavazzi, F. (2021a, December). *Emperor Commodus.* The Roman Empire. https://roman-empire.net/people/commodus/

Cavazzi, F. (2021b, December 17). *Emperor Honorius.* The Roman Empire. https://roman-empire.net/collapse/honorius/

Corletti, A. (2017, April). *Ancient eaters: Elagabalus, the Roman doctor frank-n-furter (203-222 CE).* Pass the Flamingo: Ancient Food History and Recipes.

https://passtheflamingo.com/2017/04/26/ancient-eaters-elagabalus-the-roman-doctor-frank-n-furter-203-222-ce/

Dimuro, G. (2022, November 29). *The story of mad Roman Emperor Commodus was more outrageous than "Gladiator" could depict.* All That's Interesting. https://allthatsinteresting.com/commodus

Fagan, G. (2017, December). *Intrigue, insanity, and the reign of Commodus.* Wondrium Daily. https://www.wondriumdaily.com/intrigue-insanity-reign-commodus/

Franz, G. (1999). *The king and I: The Apostle John and emperor Domitian, part 1.* Biblearchaeology.org. https://biblearchaeology.org/research/new-testament-era/3080-the-king-and-i-the-apostle-john-and-emperor-domitian-part-1

Geggel, L. (2018, September 18). *The weird reason Roman Emperors were assassinated.* Livescience.com. https://www.livescience.com/63277-roman-emperor-assassinations.html

Gill, N. S. (2019). *Elagabalus - Roman Emperor.* ThoughtCo. https://www.thoughtco.com/elagabalus-emperor-of-rome-111463

Grout, J. (n.d.). *Alma Tadema—The roses of heliogabalus.* Penelope.uchicago.edu. https://penelope.uchicago.edu/~grout/encyclopaedia_romana/severans/roses.html

Hallman, C. (2019, January 30). *The wealthiest historical figures and how much they would be worth in today's dollars.* Www.titlemax.com. https://www.titlemax.com/discovery-center/money-finance/wealthiest-historical-figures-in-todays-dollars/#:~:text=Augustus%20Caesar%20%E2%80%94%20Potentially%20the%20richest

Hansley, K. (2018, December). *Nero reportedly survived an assassination attempt because of a discarded snakeskin.* The Historian's Hut. https://thehistorianshut.com/2018/12/09/nero-reportedly-survived-an-assassination-attempt-because-of-a-discarded-snakeskin/

Hays, J. (2018, October). *Nero's cruelty, buffoonery and strange sex life.* Factsanddetails.com. https://factsanddetails.com/world/cat56/sub368/entry-6272.html

Healy, P. J. (n.d.). *Commodus.* Catholic Answers. Retrieved October 2023, from https://www.catholic.com/encyclopedia/commodus

Hoekstra, K. (2021, September). *10 facts about Emperor Domitian.* History Hit. https://www.historyhit.com/facts-about-emperor-domitian/

Hudson, M. (2016, June 9). *Emperor told Britannia to look to its own defence.* Www.ft.com. https://www.ft.com/content/6786129c-2cd6-11e6-a18d-a96ab29e3c95

Jarus, O. (2013, October). *Emperor Nero: Facts & biography.* Live Science; Live Science. https://www.livescience.com/40277-emperor-nero-facts.html

Jasiński, J. (n.d.-a). *Domitian and fears about assassination.* Imperium Romanum. Retrieved October 11, 2023, from https://imperiumromanum.pl/en/curiosities/domitian-and-fears-about-assassination/

Jasiński, J. (n.d.-b). *Quotes of Nero.* Retrieved October 7, 2023, from https://imperiumromanum.pl/en/roman-art-and-culture/golden-thoughts-of-romans/quotes-of-nero/

Jasiński, J. (2021a, February). *Usurpations in Roman Empire throughout history.* Imperium Romanum.

https://imperiumromanum.pl/en/article/usurpations-in-roman-empire-throughout-history/

Jasiński, J. (2021b, September). *Top 10 sex scandals in ancient Rome.* Imperium Romanum. https://imperiumromanum.pl/en/article/top-10-sex-scandals-in-ancient-rome/

Jesse, M. (2015, November 24). *Emperor Honorius, history's victim.* Romageddon. https://romageddon.wordpress.com/2015/11/24/emperor-honorius-historys-victim/

Johns, K. (2020a, May 4). *Elagabalus: Emperor of opposites explained.* TheCollector. https://www.thecollector.com/elagabalus/

Johns, K. (2020b, December 6). *Emeperor Commodus: Lucius Aurelius Commodus.* TheCollector. https://www.thecollector.com/facts-on-roman-emperor-commodus/

Joshua. (2020, October). *Nero, history's most despised emperor, gets a makeover.* Smithsonian Magazine. https://www.smithsonianmag.com/history/new-nicer-nero-history-roman-emperor-180975776/

MacGuill, D. (2018, July 31). *Cicero's "two thousand year old warning" about treason.* Snopes. https://www.snopes.com/fact-check/cicero-treason-quote/

Magie, D. (1921). *Historia Augusta.* Harvard University Press.

Mark, J. (2018, October 30). *Cleopatra VII.* World History Encyclopedia. https://www.worldhistory.org/Cleopatra_VII/

Mead, R. (2021, June). *How nasty was Nero, really?* The New Yorker. https://www.newyorker.com/magazine/2021/06/14/how-nasty-was-nero-really

Meddings, A. (2020, June 4). *The truth behind Caligula's Nemi ships.* Alexandermeddings.com.

https://alexandermeddings.com/history/ancient-history/caligulas-nemi-ships/

Meddings, A. (2022, March 1). *12 gruesome Roman emperor deaths: Julius Caesar to Domitian.* Alexandermeddings.com. https://alexandermeddings.com/history/roman-emperor-deaths/#Sixth_Point_Header

Medori, J. (n.d.). *Quotes for world history class unit-by-unit.* Teach 'N Thrive. Retrieved October 5, 2023, from https://teachnthrive.com/teaching-ideas/general/quotes-for-world-history-unit-by-unit/

Mijatovic, A. (2012). *A brief biography of Elagabalus: The transgender ruler of Rome.* Outhistory.org. https://outhistory.org/exhibits/show/tgi-bios/elagabalus

Mingoia, J. (2023, January 19). *The Domus Aurea, Nero's Golden Palace.* Smarthistory.org. https://smarthistory.org/domus-aurea-golden-palace/

Moore, H., & McCormick*Roman Empire*, P. (2003). Domitian (part i). *Dominitian JBS, 25.* https://biblicalstudies.org.uk/pdf/irish-biblical-studies/25-2_074.pdf

philosiblog. (2013, March 16). *It is better, of course, to know useless things than to know nothing.* Philosiblog. https://philosiblog.com/2013/03/16/it-is-better-of-course-to-know-useless-things-than-to-know-nothing/

Raghavan, J. S. (2013, March 22). *The nocturnal collectors of leftovers.* The New Indian Express. https://www.newindianexpress.com/opinions/2013/mar/22/the-nocturnal-collectors-of--leftovers-460787.html

Randle, A. (2021, September). *11 Roman emperors who helped mold the ancient world.* HISTORY. https://www.history.com/news/timeline-emperors-roman-republic

Ricketts, C. (2018, August). *The oldest obsession: Sex lives in ancient Rome.* History Hit; History Hit. https://www.historyhit.com/the-oldest-obsession-sex-lives-in-ancient-rome/

Roos, D. (2021, November 30). *The true history of Commodus, the mad emperor of ancient Rome.* HowStuffWorks. https://history.howstuffworks.com/historical-figures/commodus.htm

Sandison, A. T. (1958). The madness of the Emperor Caligula. *Medical History, 2*(3), 202–209. https://doi.org/10.1017/s0025727300023759

Sankofa, C. (2023, June 2). *Caligula quotes about the famous Caesar.* Everyday Power. https://everydaypower.com/caligula-quotes/

Suetonius, Thomson, A., & Forester, T. (2014). *The lives of the twelve Caesars.* Benediction Classics.

Thayer, B. (n.d.). *The life of Commodus.* Historia Augusta. https://penelope.uchicago.edu/Thayer/E/Roman/Texts/Historia_Augusta/Commodus*.html#note40

Tyndale. (2017). *Holy Bible: NLT study Bible.* Tyndale House Publishers.

Vermeulen, M. (2020, September). *Year of the four emperors: A complete overview.* TheCollector. https://www.thecollector.com/year-of-the-four-emperors-overview/

Wasson, D. (2013, April). *Domitian.* World History Encyclopedia. https://www.worldhistory.org/domitian/

Wasson, D. L. (2018, April). *Roman emperor.* World History Encyclopedia. https://www.worldhistory.org/Roman_Emperor/

Image References

6212079. (2017, September 6). *Marcus Aurelius, Roman emperor* [Image]. Pixabay. https://pixabay.com/photos/marcus-aurelius-roman-emperor-2721715/

ArAdAstra. (2016, December 29). *Gladiator, warrior, gear* [Image]. Pixabay. https://pixabay.com/photos/gladiator-warrior-gear-weapons-1931077/

djedj. (2018, May 24). *Hermaphrodite statue* [Image]. Pixabay. https://pixabay.com/photos/hermaphrodite-statue-marble-naked-3425193/

djedj. (2018, May 27). *Statue, sculpture, stone* [Image]. Pixabay. https://pixabay.com/photos/statue-sculpture-stone-bust-face-3434177/

elukac. (2017, January 13). *Horses, Roman, arena* [Image]. Pixabay. https://pixabay.com/photos/horses-roman-arena-historic-race-1976554/

GDJ. (2020, October 17). *Emperor leader Nero* [Image]. Pixabay. https://pixabay.com/vectors/emperor-leader-nero-roman-line-art-5660773/

GDJ. (2021, July 10). *Julia Agrippina empress sculpture* [Image]. Pixabay. https://pixabay.com/vectors/julia-agrippina-empress-sculpture-6393259/

Guapsie. (2023, August 24). *Tiberius* [Image]. Pixabay. https://pixabay.com/photos/tiberius-emperor-rome-antique-bust-8208852/

louisredon. (2019, March 7). *Caracalla bust* [Image]. Pixabay. https://pixabay.com/photos/caracalla-bust-antique-severe-4040123/

Massimo Virgilio. (2021, February 8). *Gray scale photo of man holding sword statue* [Image]. Unsplash. https://unsplash.com/photos/gray-scale-photo-of-man-holding-sword-statue-DvSUgoPoVMQ

Meelimello. (2018, March 10). *Sculpture, statue, art* [Image]. Pixabay. https://pixabay.com/photos/sculpture-statue-art-ancient-3213864/

Nick van den Berg. (2019, March 8). *Woman carrying baby statue* [Image]. Unsplash. https://unsplash.com/photos/woman-carrying-baby-statue-clip-art-GVheioPZdpk

Pixabay. (2017, July 5). *White and red rooster* [Image]. Pexels. https://www.pexels.com/photo/beak-blur-chicken-close-up-458825/

Skitterphoto. (2017, September 27). *Julius, Caesar, Roman* [Image]. Pixabay. https://pixabay.com/photos/julius-caesar-roman-italy-rome-2789915/

The_Double_A. (2017, February 1). *Colosseum, Rome* [Image]. Pixabay. https://pixabay.com/photos/colosseum-rome-italy-ancient-rome-2030639/

Thomas K. (2023, March 15). *Multiple Roman silver coins showing different Roman emperors* [Image]. Pexels. https://www.pexels.com/photo/multiple-roman-silver-coins-showing-different-roman-emperors-15954089/

Made in the USA
Monee, IL
15 June 2024

59980426R10074